GRAVEL CYCLING

 velopress®

3002 Sterling Circle, Suite 100
Boulder, CO 80301–2338 USA

VeloPress is the leading publisher of books on endurance sports. Focused on cycling, triathlon, running, swimming, and nutrition/diet, VeloPress books help athletes achieve their goals of going faster and farther. Preview books and contact us at velopress.com.

Distributed in the United States and Canada by Ingram Publisher Services

Library of Congress Cataloging-in-Publication Data
Legan, Nick, author.
Gravel cycling: the complete guide to gravel racing and adventure
     bikepacking / Nick Legan.
Boulder, Colorado: VeloPress, [2017] | Includes
     bibliographical references and index.
LCCN 2017021191 | ISBN 9781937715700 (alk. paper)
LCSH: Cycling. | Bicycle racing. | Gravel roads—Recreational use.
LCC GV1041 .L435 2017 | DDC 796.6—dc23

This paper meets the requirements of ANSI/NISO Z39.48-1992 (Permanence of Paper).

17   18   19 / 10   9   8   7   6   5   4   3   2   1

GRAVEL CYCLING

The Complete Guide to Gravel Racing and Adventure Bikepacking

NICK LEGAN

 Boulder, Colorado

The roots of gravel riding run deep in the Midwest. Here adventurous souls take on the Almanzo 100 in Minnesota.

To my parents, Paul and Mary, whose unwavering love gave me the confidence to seek out adventures both close to home and farther afield.

And to Kristen, my smiling partner through all the peaks and valleys of life.

The roads outside of Beaver, Utah, offer incredible scenery, fast descents, and tortuous climbs.

CONTENTS

Clayton Wangbichler
makes his way through
a tight section on the
Tahoe Rim Trail in
northern California.

GRAVEL GRINDERS

DOMESTIC

(1) Grasshopper Adventure Series

Sonoma County, CA
January–June

PAGE 22

(2) Land Run

Stillwater, OK
March

PAGE 28

(3) Barry-Roubaix

Hastings, MI
April

PAGE 34

(4) Trans Iowa

Grinnell, IA
April

PAGE 40

(5) Almanzo

Spring Valley, MN
May

PAGE 46

(6) Dirty Kanza

Emporia, KS
May or June

PAGE 52

(7) Crusher in the Tushar

Beaver, UT
July

PAGE 58

(8) Gravel Worlds

Lincoln, NE
August

PAGE 66

(9) Deerfield Dirt Road Randonnée

Deerfield, MA
August

PAGE 72

(10) Rebecca's Private Idaho

Ketchum, ID
September

PAGE 78

(11) Grinduro

Quincy, CA
October

PAGE 84

INTERNATIONAL

ADVENTURE BIKEPACKING

MULTIDAY ROUTES

**① Great Divide
Mountain Bike Route**

Banff, AB to Antelope Wells, NM | 2,768 miles

PAGE 142

② Denali Highway

Paxson, AK to Cantwell, AK | 135 miles

PAGE 158

③ Trans North California

Reno, NV to Mendocino, CA | 400 miles

PAGE 164

④ Oregon Outback

Klamath Falls, OR to the Deschutes River | 364 miles

PAGE 170

⑤ Katy Trail

Clinton, MO to Machens, MO | 237 miles

PAGE 176

**⑥ Great Allegheny Passage
and C&O Towpath**

Pittsburgh, PA to Washington, D.C. | 335 miles

PAGE 182

SINGLETRACK
MULTIDAY ROUTES

① Colorado Trail

Waterton Canyon, CO to Durango, CO | 525 miles

PAGE 190

② Arizona Trail

Sierra Vista, AZ to Kaibab Plateau, AZ | 739 miles

PAGE 198

WA

OR

AK

N

CA

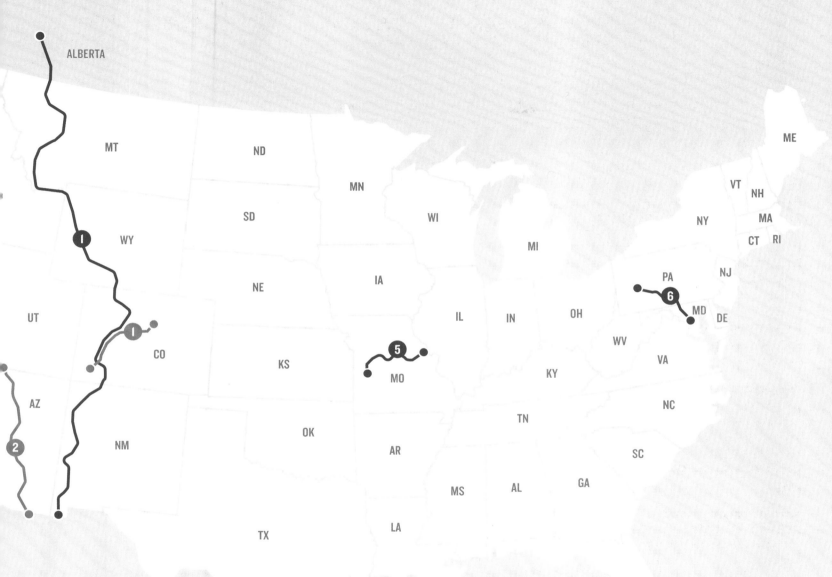

Attaching your number plate makes it official. This one's from the Crusher in the Tushar.

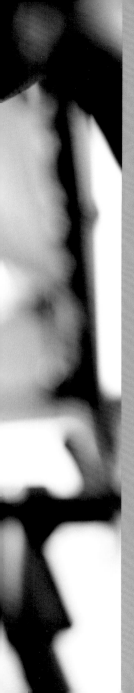

① GETTING STARTED

Paused at the side of what few would consider a road, the morning sun still low on the horizon, I was struck by the beauty of the setting I had just entered. Rolling green hills covered in tall grass were bisected by a narrow brown path of dirt and gravel. Clusters of cows dotted the land, while small white clouds floated through a brightening blue sky. The humid air carried a sweetness that would soon burn off in the Midwest's intense summer heat. An ant-like procession of multicolored Lycra-clad cyclists labored their way out of view ahead. Looking back, hundreds more bobbing cyclists made their way in my direction. As they approached me, they called out to ask if I needed anything.

Returning my bottle to the cage after a swig of water, my eyes fell on the number plate attached to my handlebars. This served as a helpful reminder that despite the idyllic setting and friendly nature of the other cyclists nearby, I was in a race, my first gravel race. My first double century, or 200-mile ride, in fact. Somewhere in the beautifully brutal Flint Hills of Kansas, a couple hours into the 2011 Dirty Kanza 200, I fell in love with gravel racing.

In the ensuing years, having made my way to other events around the United States, the love affair has only grown more intense. I'm certainly not alone, and that's the whole point. In searching for your own limits at gravel events, you find a family of people seeking untapped abilities. The shared suffering of trudging through miles of mud and hours of chilly progress against headwinds brings cyclists together.

And just as social media makes discovering new gravel events easier, it also makes staying connected with your new gravel brothers and sisters more convenient. Online, just as at the starting line or when out on nearly forgotten dirt roads, the gravel community supports its members, inspiring them to gather repeatedly for new adventures, new terrain, new vistas. It is a self-perpetuating circle of curiosity, preparation, testing, dissecting, and trying again.

For those who prefer solitude to competition, gravel roads offer escape from the increasingly busy paved roads around the world. Cyclists are discovering that riding on dirt lanes and gravel roads is the calmest form of cycling, a way to escape the hustle and bustle of daily life. Jim Cummins, the founder of the Dirty Kanza 200, embraces the term *gravel grinder*, but for a different reason than you might think. It's not because the ride is a grind—not at all. It's because going out and riding gravel allows him to leave the grind of daily life behind.

Bikepacking offers even more joys, a long-form escape into a world you may not have seen before. Imagine extending your gravel ride with some nights under the stars, and you will discover a joyous time in nature—self-supported, self-reliant, and richly fulfilling.

For new cyclists, riding gravel and solitary dirt roads is a natural solution to the problems of road riding or mountain biking. Traffic on paved roads scares many new cyclists, and the absence of a safe shoulder or the threatening presence of a gutter strewn with broken glass and debris can be paralyzing. The technical skills required for mountain biking are also an impediment for many. Riding gravel and dirt roads, on the other hand, offers a quiet cycling experience with only a minimal amount of cycling prowess required.

The remoteness of gravel roads also helps produce better cyclists, riders with a sense of self-reliance. Many gravel races reinforce this by requiring competitors to self-support using convenience stores found along the race route. This is a far cry from the world of Tour de France racing, where a team car is ready at a moment's notice to deliver food, clothing, even a spare bike if needed. In contrast, gravel race promoters borrow race rules from the roots of mountain bike racing, where making it to the finish line requires fitness and self-reliance, as well as thoughtful riding to preserve your bicycle. In addition to making the organization of an event a much simpler affair, this approach creates cyclists who are unlikely to find themselves marooned by mechanical or nutritional problems.

In short, gravel riding has a lot to offer to cyclists of any ilk. A full day exploring farm roads or mountainous miners' paths

Bailey Newbrey and
Allison Zmuda kick
up dust as they power
through an early morning
section of Dirty Kanza

Fast-rolling tires are the way to go for Almanzo, held in Spring Valley, Minnesota, every May.

29980

will bring highs and lows, flat tires and new friends. These roads are much more than a venue for cycling. They serve as romantic reminders of bygone eras while also inspiring an adventurous future for the sport.

Where did gravel riding come from?

Gravel cycling is the original form of cycling. Modern gravel riders are simply rediscovering the sport's roots. When bicycles first became popular in the mid-19th century, almost all roads worldwide were dirt. Although asphalt roads existed as early as 615 B.C.E. in Babylon, they didn't become common outside of city centers until the 20th century. In the United States, much of the impetus to pave roads came from the League of American Wheelmen (now known as the League of American Bicyclists). Formed in 1880, the group advocated for improving road conditions, and its efforts led to the creation of the National Highway System.

Fortunately for modern gravel riders, the league was not 100 percent successful. The U.S. Department of Transportation, in a 2013 report, noted that nearly 1.4 million miles of the country's 4 million miles of public roads are unpaved. With well over a quarter of our public roads made of dirt and gravel, opportunities abound.

As with many organic developments, the modern incarnation of gravel riding was simply a matter of cyclists in rural areas taking advantage of the miles and miles of remote farm and mountain roads they had on hand. A pragmatic sense of using what you have at your disposal is the very heart of gravel riding. Seeking out unpaved routes allows riders to avoid increasingly busy paved roads, where many only find anxiety and motorists intent on texting. Depending on your location, riding gravel also bypasses the need to build a trail network, which mountain biking often requires.

What is a gravel bike?

Simply put, a gravel bike is a bicycle that you ride on gravel. This definition is intentionally vague because riders all over the world enjoy riding dirt and gravel on bicycles as different as lightweight carbon-fiber road race bikes and heavy-duty dual-suspension mountain bikes. Because surfaces and terrain differ so greatly, what's best for you in your area can require a bit of experimentation. As you'll see in this book's photos, the diversity of bicycles used for gravel riding is startling and inventive.

In many cases, buying a new bike is not required. At the same time, a new steed may serve your needs better than what you currently own and add to your on-bike fun. Later, we'll explore how to upgrade your current bicycle for gravel as well as give you a quick primer on what to look for if you decide to pull the trigger on a new bike. Rest assured, though, that a big investment is not needed. The only requirement for gravel biking is your willingness to take on new adventures.

What skills do you need to go gravel riding?

A bonus to gravel riding is that it doesn't require a high level of rider skill like mountain biking does. It has a low barrier of entry to a good time aboard a bike in a beautiful rural setting.

That's not to say that gravel biking doesn't require attentive and careful riding, especially when cornering. But you can easily achieve those skills, and thanks to the quiet nature of most gravel and dirt roads, the classroom setting is not harried. Small bobbles don't put you in a lane of constant traffic or careening off a narrow trail into rocks and trees.

Riding on loose surfaces can be unnerving at first. But with some instruction and a bit of practice, riding on gravel will raise your skill level across the board, with those skills then translating to road and mountain biking. Much like a road rider on the lookout for glass and potholes, a good gravel cyclist is continually scanning ahead, looking for the smoothest path, wary of deep patches of loose gravel, and aware of what little traffic may be approaching. We become students of roads, judging if standing over a rise is a good idea or if it will result in a spinning rear wheel. We memorize the location of washboard sections and revel in mastering particularly rough roads.

Because most dirt and gravel roads are maintained annually by state and county agencies, we get to experience them anew after additional gravel is laid or grading work is completed. Rain, snow, wind, and traffic also continually evolve a gravel road's surface. All this rewards the attentive rider and provides subtly different roads week by week, keeping the riding fresh for riders who have limited access to gravel roads.

Give it a go

With a strong emphasis on fun, gravel may be the shining light in cycling's future. It mostly bypasses interactions with motorists and sidesteps the access issues associated with mountain biking. Riding gravel doesn't require special equipment or a high skill level. With so many opportunities to ride gravel and so few impediments to giving it a try, there's no reason for the growth of gravel cycling to slow.

Our next chapter contains an introduction to gravel racing, but bear in mind that you don't need to compete to ride gravel. Cycling as a sport has a strong tradition in competition, a tradition that sometimes overshadows the simple pleasures of freedom and exploration that riding a bike can deliver.

Make no excuses for how you ride, be it fast or slow, long or short. Just ride.

Pavement, dirt, singletrack: California's Grinduro features a little bit of everything.

The calm before the storm at the Deerfield Dirt Road Randonnée in Franklin County, Massachusetts.

② RACE PREP

For those who have discovered gravel riding and now have the itch to compete, gravel races dot the globe, offering a wide variety of distances, elevations, surfaces, and local cultures. Don't be intimidated by the fact that numbers are issued and times are taken. Without fail, gravel race promoters foster an inclusive atmosphere that welcomes riders of all abilities. Racers too are extremely encouraging, offering aid to riders in need and cheering each other on as the hours tick by.

Many races focus on creating a festival vibe, with live music, main street parties, and barbeques and beer at the finish line. With strong roots in mountain bike race promotion, many race organizers actively cultivate a casual, family-friendly environment at their events. The communities, meanwhile—typically small towns with easy access to alluring gravel roads—seize the opportunity to host racers and their families. After attending some races year after year, racers often develop a sense of a homecoming when returning to perennial venue towns. This is thanks to the down-home feel but also to the people you invariably meet who race the gravel circuit, seeking new challenges and a sense of belonging.

Preparing for your first event

If you feel like you're ready to join the gravel racing tribe (fear not, there are no initiation rites in this gang), then bravo! The hardest part is often simply making the decision to give it a go.

Be sure to do some homework before heading to your first event. Informed planning can go a long way toward your success. Seek help. It can come from a coach, more-experienced riding buddies, gravel forums, and past participants. If you have event-specific questions, contact the race promoter after reading the rules and racers' bible, both typically available online. Be up-front, mention your newbie status, and, as Basil King said, "Mighty forces will come to your aid." A lack of experience is never something to be embarrassed about. By taking part, you're looking to gain experience. It's an opportunity, not a hindrance.

As you prepare for your race, don't feel that you have to undertake rides that equal the distance and elevation gain you'll encounter on race day. If you do have the opportunity to get out for a race-distance ride, of course you should go for it. It will give you a confidence boost and point out any problems that might arise in the final miles of a long ride. Just be sure that you don't fatigue yourself too close to your event.

If you're time crunched, however, a good rule of thumb is to be able to comfortably complete 75 percent of what you'll ride on race day. For example, if you're signed up for a gravel century (100 miles), be sure you have ridden 75 miles in similar conditions, with a similar proportion of climbing to the amount you'll encounter on the big day. The adrenaline and extra excitement you'll experience during the race will usually push you through the other 25 percent with energy to spare. Don't underestimate your willpower.

In the months before your date with destiny, take notes after each training ride that cover what worked and what disappointed. Whether you write them on paper or save them on your phone, checklists serve as insurance and a quick reference. Was that new drink mix a success or a recipe for a sour stomach? Did lower tire pressure work well for you or lead to a series of pinch flats? Try to be systematic in your approach so you don't have to learn important lessons multiple times. As your notes grow, you can begin to develop a race day plan for your hydration, nutrition, and bike setup. The more decisions you can make before leaving for the race, the better.

It doesn't hurt to do a couple of race day simulations, a.k.a. dress rehearsals, during your buildup. Load up your bike with all the food, drink, spares, inflation gear, and tools you plan to carry on race day. Go for a good, long ride. Did anything rattle loose?

Cheers greet wet conditions at the Land Run 100 start line in Stillwater, Oklahoma.

Getting organized

Arriving at the race check-in parking lot, you exit your car and stretch for a minute before heading to a pop-up tent to collect your race number and route maps. Back at the car, you unload your bike, pump the tires, and load up your bottles and race food. That done, you grab your bag full of clothing and your helmet. Walking to the public restrooms nearby, you change into your jersey and shorts, and lather on the sunscreen. Back at the car, you put on your helmet and sunglasses, then reach inside your bag for your shoes, coming away with only air and bewilderment. Your shoes! You frantically check the rest of the car, eventually dumping the contents of your bag on the ground. With little hope, you backtrack to the check-in tent and the restrooms. No luck. You've forgotten them at home, a three-hour drive away. Despondent, you weigh your options. None of them includes racing today.

We've all done this or something similar. And it's usually only after missing a race or a group ride that we decide to get organized. A race day packing list can save

Lay out your gear before you go to make sure you have at least one of everything you will need. Not shown here but nice to have: an extra pair of clean, dry socks for afterward. Nothing's worse than standing around in cold, wet feet after a race.

heartache and worry. Build one out as you ready yourself for your training rides, far in advance of your event. Think of all the separate pieces you collect before each ride. Write them down. (Ideally, keep them all in one location in your house, making it easier to get out the door with everything on a regular basis.)

Consider clothing needs first, head to toe. Helmet, hat, sunglasses, neck gaiter (if it's cold), base layer, jersey, arm warmers, gloves, vest, jacket, shorts, knee or leg warmers, socks, shoes, shoe covers. Maybe you like to wear a wristband for sweat. Write that down. Perhaps you like to pull on waterproof oversocks when it rains. Write that down. You get the point.

Some suggest making multiple lists based on different weather conditions. This can be useful, but weather can be unpredictable. It's best to bring too much clothing to the start and leave it in the car instead of being caught off guard by a freak storm.

After clothing, think about food and hydration. Will the race have a drop bag system, allowing you to prepack items for later in the race and have them delivered to aid stations? If so, assemble your bag or bags while you're still at home, calm and collected. You'll do a better job and eliminate a potentially stressful task the night before the race. Better to relax with a book or catch up with friends.

Next, consider your bike. Always take along a rag, chain lube, and a floor pump. You can leave the repair stand at home, because in your efforts to eliminate pre-race stress, you paid for a tune-up (or did one yourself) before leaving for the race. Make sure that your on-bike repair kit is ready to go. Did you replace the tube in your seat bag after that last flat? What about the CO_2 cartridge? Do you have a multi-tool, tire lever, spare chain link, and any other small parts you like to carry?

Be methodical in your approach to readiness and your race performances will improve. Ridding yourself of last-minute woes allows you to focus on the effort ahead and take better care of pre-race nutrition and hydration.

Did your bottles eject from their cages on the first rough section of road? Did your seat pack rattle, slowly driving you insane? Small items can have a big impact on your race results. Addressing them early can remove them as variables in the gravel racing equation.

Pre-race bike tune-up

A couple of weeks before the race, give your trusty steed some love. If you're not mechanically inclined, take your bike to your local shop. Tell them what's on the horizon. Install new tires, if needed. Also be sure the brake pads and drivetrain are in good working order. They don't need to be new, just functioning efficiently. Be sure to ask for a bolt check too. Putting in lots

A clean drivetrain will make your bike faster and costs nothing but a bit of time.

of miles on rough roads can vibrate bolts loose. You'll want to be confident that a water bottle cage isn't about to fall off, for example. Thread-locking compounds such as Loctite are great for use on bolts that are rarely adjusted. Be sure to use a midlevel compound, Blue 242 in the case of Loctite. Compounds that offer increased retention, such as Loctite's Green 290, require the application of heat to loosen the bolt—no good if you need to fix something in the middle of a race.

Regarding the rest of the bike, don't install anything new this close to your event unless something is broken. You want tried-and-true equipment for your race. Discovering 50 miles into a race that a new saddle, grips, handlebar, or other component is not working properly can ruin your results. If you are curious about a new wonder product, test it thoroughly during training. Race day should be about exploring your physical limits, not your equipment's.

Then get in several rides before you leave for your event to ensure that all is working optimally. New shift cables can stretch after a ride or two, leading to inconsistent shifting. Sometimes tubeless tires can take a little bit of trail time to seal fully. You want to eliminate all of these potential stress inducers before you pack for the race.

Closer to race day, wash your bike, or at least wipe it down. A clean drivetrain is one of the cheapest ways to make your bike go faster. With everything running smoothly,

Aid stations, like Deerfield's, are not always provided; check the rules before you go.

you won't waste energy to overcome the drag of a gritty, grimy cassette, chain, derailleur, and crank.

Clean the chain as best you can (it's smart to wear dishwashing gloves and a shop apron during this process). A splash of degreaser on a rag will help strip the grease and oil from a chain, carrying away grit and grime in the process.

Even better is a small stiff-bristled brush dipped in degreaser, which not only applies the degreaser but can also get to crevices inside the chain plates, front and rear derailleurs, cassette, and chainrings. Bike shops sell brushes made specifically for this purpose, or you can buy a small 2-inch paintbrush from the hardware store. If you decide to use this method, you need to rinse the drivetrain thoroughly afterwards, using a garden hose. (Avoid pressure washers at all costs, as they can

force degreaser into bearings.) Once you've scrubbed and rinsed the drivetrain, you may as well wash the rest of the bike while you have it outside and the hose is hooked up. See the sidebar "Bike washing 101" for quick step-by-step instructions. Once the bike is dry, lube the chain, check your work, and you're ready to go.

Know the race rules

After reading the race rules, read them again. Be sure that you understand them. I emphasize this because gravel races can differ quite a bit from event to event. Some are old-school, completely do-it-yourself affairs, with the only support coming in the form of convenience stores along the route. Organizers will give racers a rough idea of how many miles they'll ride between opportunities to resupply. Other than that, it's up to participants to consider

Bike washing 101

Supply list:
- repair stand
- bucket
- garden hose
- sponges
- brushes
- degreaser brush
- dish soap
- degreaser
- clean rags
- polish
- chain lube

1 GATHER YOUR SUPPLIES.
Fill a bucket with warm soapy water. Dawn dish soap works well. Buy a sponge and brush kit from a local shop, or assemble one yourself. Tampico fiber brushes are best, as they don't retain grease. For sponges, I like those made for masonry work. Cut them in half. Use one for the drivetrain, the other for the rest of your bike.

2 REMOVE ACCESSORIES.
Lights, computers, pumps, seat bags—take them all off.

3 MAKE A BRUSH BUCKET.
Cut the top off an old water bottle just below the point where it is widest.

Pour in a small amount of degreaser. Pedro's Oranj Peelz, Muc-Off Bio Degreaser, and Finish Line Citrus Degreaser are my favorites. Put your bike in the stand and stick the degreaser cup in the water bottle cage on the seat tube. Using a stiff paintbrush or cog brush, paint degreaser on all of the drivetrain parts, paying special attention to both sides of the chain, chainrings, the gaps in the cassette, and the pulleys on the rear derailleur. Let it soak in. Then return to each part, scrubbing with the same paintbrush. Avoid applying degreaser to disc brakes!

4 RINSE. Spray off the scrubbed drivetrain with a garden hose on low pressure. Stand on the non-driveside (left side), spraying the drivetrain from the back so that grease, grit, and grime are rinsed off the bike instead of simply transferred to the other side.

5 CHECK YOUR WORK. If you missed some spots, hit the drivetrain with degreaser again. Rinse once again.

6 REMOVE THE WHEELS.

7 WASH WITH SOAP. Wash everything from top to bottom, back to front. Use the sponge reserved for non-drivetrain parts to wash the saddle and the saddle's underside, down the seatpost and around the rear triangle. Switch to your drivetrain sponge and run it over the derailleurs, cranks, pedals, and chain. Switch back to your frame sponge for the front triangle, handlebars, and fork. Move on to the wheels. Check for loose spokes while wiping each one. Hit the tires, sidewalls, rims, and hubs.

8 RINSE WITH THE HOSE.
Give everything a close inspection, checking for dirt as well as cracks, dents, blemishes, cuts in the tires, worn brake pads, frayed cables, and so on.

9 DRY. Let the bike drip-dry in the sun, if possible, for some time while you put away the hose and dump out the wash bucket. Returning to the bike, bounce the wheels to remove excess water. Then dry the bike with clean rags, performing a final inspection as you go. Once dry, spray polish on a clean rag and wipe down the frame and fork. Avoid the disc brake rotors and pads as well as the brake pads and braking surfaces on rim-brake bicycles.

10 LUBE THE CHAIN. Reinstall the wheels. Wipe the chain to remove any remaining water and grease. Using clean areas on your rag, continue wiping until the rag comes away clean. Then apply your preferred chain lube as instructed by the manufacturer.

their needs, carry enough supplies for the opening section, and have a credit card to pay for food and drink later in the day. For many, this is very appealing. It's a leveler of sorts. For promoters, it also places the burden on the participants, making the race organization quite a bit easier. As long as all parties are happy, there is no need to change.

Other races have aid stations stocked with fruit, pretzels, boiled potatoes (at Rebecca's Private Idaho race), energy bars, drinks, and even mechanical support in some cases. You simply show up and race. Everything else is covered.

Some events, like the Dirty Kanza 200, land somewhere in the middle. While you don't have to rely on convenience stores for resupply, the race doesn't provide assistance with food or drink. Racers are required to bring a support crew along to help at checkpoints, and only at checkpoints. They can't be out on the course unless their racer has dropped out of the race and they're heading to collect that person. There are also neutral mechanics at checkpoints who will help any participant with bike issues.

To discover these details, it's important to read through race rules carefully. There is no right or wrong way to organize a race, simply differences often born of common sense. For instance, it doesn't make sense to allow support crews on a gravel racecourse to assist racers. A car rumbling along creates a lot of dust and ruins the rural setting. Likewise, at Rebecca's Private

Eat real food: These Chocolate Quinoa Energy Balls are from Matt Kadey's book *Rocket Fuel*.

Idaho, the route is a lollipop shape, with very few access roads. So Rebecca Rusch, the event's promoter, simply supports all the racers on the course with established aid tents stocked with necessities.

Race day nutrition and hydration plan

Once you understand the level of support you can expect, it's time to develop your strategy for hydration and nutrition. Take terrain and weather conditions into account. With favorable winds, good roads, and a flat course, 25 miles can take a little over an hour. With a series of mountain passes, loose gravel, and scorching heat, 25 miles can take over three hours. Usually, expected duration is a better predictor of needs than distance. Consider all these factors when making decisions on your caloric intake and fluid needs.

Yuri Hauswald, the 2015 champion of Dirty Kanza 200, works for the sports nutrition company GU Energy Labs and has some helpful tips on fueling:

A nutrition plan for an all-day gravel session can take many forms (gels, solids, liquids) and is usually a highly personal/unique menu, as what works for one may not work for another. Choosing the incorrect foods, eating too much or too little, or eating at the wrong time can result in less than optimal performance. Nobody wants that. As corny as it might sound, fueling for a long day on the bike is like putting the correct grade gasoline in your car, and then managing the fuel levels. The better the fuel, the better the performance.

In training, you'll want to figure out exactly what to drink. In almost all cases, sports nutrition experts recommend sports drinks in lieu of plain water. The salts in sports drinks help your body retain the fluids you drink to replace what you're losing in sweat. Some sports drinks focus solely on hydration, aiming to replenish both fluids and the minerals and electrolytes you lose through perspiration.

Other drink mixes contain electrolytes but also provide calories. These tend to be a bit heavier on the stomach, so you'll want to experiment during training to find what works best for you. One drink mix may be a one-way ticket to a sour stomach while you can happily drink another for hours on end. When you find one you like, take notes on

how much you can comfortably consume per hour and even the number of scoops you're using per bottle. This information will help you build your race day plan.

Similarly, you'll want to test out different foods while riding. Some cyclists go with a "real food" diet, eating small sandwiches, fruit, homemade energy bars, and the like. They'll combine this with an electrolyte drink. Skratch Labs, a leader in sports nutrition, promotes this model, encouraging athletes to drink their hydration and eat their calories.

Some cyclists prefer to drink a higher calorie solution and supplement it with additional food, be it gels, energy bars, or some other preferred food. It all depends on what your gastrointestinal tract can handle while riding. Additionally, what is possible for you to digest on a cold day can be different from a hot day. During an easy day on the bike, your stomach may never present an issue. Harder rides typically pose more of a problem. So experiment in conditions similar to those at your event as much as possible. And be sure to take notes on food selections that worked for you as well as foods to avoid.

Once you have tested hydration and nutrition methods, start to think about your needs on race day. It's difficult to create hard-and-fast rules, as riders vary drastically in their caloric expenditure and efficiency as well as in how much fluid they will lose during a given effort. It's worth speaking with a nutritionist or dietician if

Be sure to try a variety of drink mixes before race day so you'll know what works.

Fueling up at Dirty Kanza, where a support crew is allowed to help out at checkpoints.

you have specific questions regarding your personal needs. But try to think in terms of consumption per hour. Again, duration is usually a better metric than distance. Then create a plan of what you'll need for each section of the race.

In my case, I try to eat 300 to 400 calories per hour, with 100 grams of carbohydrates per hour. I also try to consume 24 ounces of hydration drink mix per hour, usually from Skratch Labs or Osmo Nutrition. In some cases, I'll carry

one bottle of GU's Roctane, a high-calorie sports mix, to get in liquid calories in the event that solid foods aren't sitting well. I typically have a mix of food items on hand so I can follow my stomach's fancy instead of forcing myself to eat unappetizing energy bars. Based on those figures and average speed estimates, it's pretty simple to develop a nutrition plan.

If you can send drop bags ahead or if you have a support crew on hand, you can create a spreadsheet for your crew to

reference as they prepare bags for each section. Read the labels on your favorite ride foods and drinks, and ensure that you send ahead enough of both to keep you moving forward.

A great trick that my wife taught me is to incentivize yourself by putting your favorite flavors of ride foods or little treats in your later drop bags. You'll have something to look forward to while you make your way forward. They are an almost literal carrot enticing you to push harder.

One last reminder: Race day experimentation rarely goes well. No matter what a new product claims or a trusted friend recommends, unless you've tested it for yourself, you're better off avoiding it.

Navigation

Race navigation can vary widely as well. Some promoters carefully mark the entire course with signs, stakes, and spray paint. They may include maps of the course in your race packet. Some will upload a GPX file, an open-format electronic file that shows waypoints, tracks, and routes, and can be installed on a GPS device, thus offering turn-by-turn directions. Modern GPS computers from Garmin, Wahoo, Lezyne, and others offer this feature on their more expensive models. You'll need to use the manufacturer's software, be it Garmin's BaseCamp or Wahoo's in-phone application, to upload the navigation file to your device.

Other promoters offer cue sheets—written turn-by-turn directions—requiring riders to remain acutely aware of their location on the course at all times. Some race promoters offer only the first set of cue sheets, which describe directions to the first checkpoint. Once a racer completes that first section of the course in the allotted time, he or she then receives the next set of cues to the next checkpoint. And so on goes the race. This complicates the affair quite a lot, as it means that you don't know how long you'll go in a particular direction, perhaps while dealing with a headwind. Metering one's effort becomes tough to assess. It's all part of the joy of racing this sort of event!

In any case, you'll want to make sure that you have either a GPS unit or a calibrated cycling computer on your bike. Measuring distance is a big part of navigation. If you can't do that reliably, it's hard to stay on any course.

COURSE MARKING
If the event you've signed up for will have a marked course, be sure to find out what those markings will be. In some cases, wooden stakes with ribbons will mark a turn. A stake on the right side of the road means turn right. A stake on the left means turn left. No stake? Carry on going straight ahead. Often a confirmation stake after a corner will let you know that you went the right way.

Some race organizers spend the money to make signs with arrows that they'll place on the course. Especially in races with several distance options, signs will mark where courses diverge. Pay close attention to pre-race briefings. It's okay to take notes. The act of writing something down can help you remember it, even if you don't attach the note to your bike.

Looks like a 747 and flies like one too: Fast racers need to master navigation.

The printed elevation profile for the Gravel Fondo offers a handy preview of what's to come.

MAPS

If an event doesn't have a marked course but provides a course map, you'll want to have an easy way to look at the map to verify you're on course. Ideally, your map holder should be somewhat waterproof, as creek crossings and rain can make some printed maps run, rendering them useless. The simplest solution is to put the map in a plastic bag. SealLine and Aloksak both offer great map cases that will last longer than Ziploc-type bags. Check camping stores for clear map cases too.

Then you'll need a way of clipping that map to your bars. Look to touring cyclists for advice here. CueClip makes a set of clips that are installed using Velcro loops. These are an especially versatile way to clamp your notes and maps; they work on drop bars, flat bars, and aerobars.

Some racers make their own map holders using sheets of plastic, office supply binder clips made for large stacks of paper, and zip ties to hold them in place. As with nutrition, it's best to experiment with your chosen navigation system in training.

GPX FILES

If you're going to use a GPX file and a GPS to make your way around a course, be sure to familiarize yourself with how to load a track onto your device and then use it to navigate. Race day is not the best time to power up everything for the first time. Personally, I prefer to switch off the turn-by-turn warnings and stick with an on-screen track. I then turn on the "off course" alarm so that I'm alerted if I make a wrong turn but don't hear the constant beeping that indicates approaching turns. But that's my preference. Figure out what works best for you.

CUE SHEETS

As with maps, if you'll be required to follow a set of cue sheets, you'll want to make sure you have some practice using the system you develop. A cue sheet holder can often be smaller than a map holder. A way to change cues quickly is also handy. Again, office supply binder clips are useful. If you prefer to buy something ready-made, Banjo Brothers offers a cue sheet holder made for cycling.

You'll want to be extra sure that your cycling computer, if you're using one, is calibrated and accurate when navigating with cue sheets. If you're using a GPS to measure the miles you cover, you should be in good shape, as they typically display distances accurate enough for cue sheet navigation.

Focus is required when racing or riding via cue sheet navigation. You can't afford to lose track of where you are or what's ahead. If you do make a mistake, you'll add the headache of having to do continual math to align the distance on your computer with the cue sheet indications. Many people use online route-building sites like Ride with GPS to design rides in their area. This site can output cue sheets. Use these to practice your navigational skills and on-bike system. Best of luck out there!

The top tube's a useful place for a stick-on cue sheet, whether homemade or supplied by the race.

An early morning chill starts the day at Grinduro. Be ready for a variety of conditions at any race.

③ ONE-DAY DOMESTIC EVENTS

There is no substitute for experience. But when considering or preparing for an event, getting a leg up by gathering the most information you can is always useful. Because races vary drastically, with different types of gravel, navigational needs, available support, distances, and terrain subtleties, here is a cheat sheet, in chronological order, of 11 popular events around the United States. This is by no means a comprehensive list of races—new events seem to pop up every month—but it does feature well-established races in different areas of the country. You'll find advice from the organizers as well as past winners. What bike to bring, tires of choice, gearing recommendations, and tips on race nutrition are also covered.

Grasshopper Adventure Series

Sonoma County, California | January–June

For almost two decades, Miguel Crawford has organized his Grasshopper Adventure Series in Sonoma County, California. While not technically races, these events, usually six per year, are extremely challenging and require participants to choose their bikes, tires, and gearing carefully. Born out of a desire to explore the rarely used roads and trails of Northern California, Crawford and his group of cohorts pieced together the hardest rides they could imagine. As word spread, the events grew; they are now well-attended rides that host legendary exploits. Crawford's event names—Old Caz, Super Sweetwater, Super Skaggs Gravel, and King Ridge Dirt Supreme—inspire joy and fear in the hearts of riders. But they also give cyclists an opportunity to test their mettle in Sonoma County.

The course shown here is Old Caz from 2017.

DEFINING FEATURES

- Home to some of California's best vineyards; extending your trip to sample the area's food and drink is worthwhile.
- The series offers a wide variety of road conditions and climbing.
- A relaxed atmosphere encourages riders to ride as hard as they like.

ESSENTIAL GEAR

- Hard to nail this down, as the courses vary a lot, but low gears and good brakes always help.
- Carry sufficient spare inner tubes, a multi-tool, and a reliable pump.

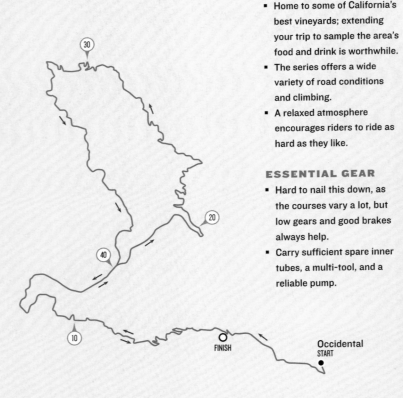

The Grasshopper Series takes in the most beautiful and challenging roads in Sonoma County, California.

A group rollout covers an early pavement section (above). Later the going gets significantly tougher (right).

California's Grasshopper Series
has been challenging adventure
riders with its mixed-surface
events for nearly two decades.

Promoter Miguel Crawford makes bike choice
intentionally difficult. Creek crossings are easier
aboard a mountain bike, but road or gravel tires
will shine on pavement.

For a dose of the best riding
that northern California has
to offer, simply sign up for
one of Crawford's Grasshopper
Series events.

Miguel Crawford

Grasshopper Series
promoter

"General fitness and bike handling are important. You also need to learn to take care of yourself at races, even if you have support. A big part of cycling's appeal to me was learning to fix things on my own."

"Old Caz has been won [by Geoff Kabush] on a mountain bike with full knobbies. It was also won by a guy named Justin Morgan on a road bike with 25mm tires. It's been won numerous times on cross bike setups. Ultimately, it comes down to the rider."

Ted King

Past winner of King Ridge
Dirt Supreme

"Starting in the town of Occidental, a hippie town in western Sonoma, I rode a Cannondale Slate stock with fat, slick tires. The event starts with a big descent, and I thought I was on the wrong bike. But thankfully, it regrouped, and I felt better about my bike choice. On a fire road climb, I put in an attack and managed to win."

"No bike is perfect. And no matter what you're on, you'll question your decision at some point."

"I was with people who knew the course well, and the course is pretty well marked without being obnoxious. There was chalk on the road."

"You're supposed to pay $20 for SAG support. I thought that was crazy. But in the end, it was the best $20 I've spent."

"It's short enough that you want to go self-supported. At the finish, there are coolers of beer, potato chips, and mixed nuts. It was awesome."

"Prepare for the worst, hope for the best. But you're not far from help if you do have a catastrophic meltdown."

"For gearing, I think the Slate is awesome, stock with a 44 up front and a 10–42 cassette in the rear. It's perfect for the Grasshopper Series."

Ted King, a former pro road racer, has taken a liking to gravel.

Land Run

Stillwater, Oklahoma | March

Stillwater, Oklahoma, is home to District Bicycles, a local bike shop, and the magic that owners Bobby and Crystal Wintle create with their enthusiastic love of gravel cycling. Whether it's through the rowdy but fun weekly group rides or the after-hours custom bike build parties, the Wintles spread excitement for bikes and riding them on gravel. In a very short time, they've created a culture of cycling, good times, and inclusive camaraderie.

Their race, the Land Run, offers cyclists a look at the red dirt roads of rural Oklahoma. Importantly, if rain falls, as it often can in mid-March, those roads become a sticky clay concoction that is infamous for its ability to destroy drivetrains. Be sure you're ready for some hike-a-bike, as it's sometimes the only way to move forward on the course without ending your day with a mechanical issue.

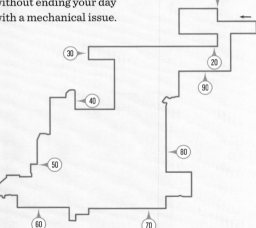

DEFINING FEATURES

- Stillwater, in northeast Oklahoma, is the home of Oklahoma State University and the National Wrestling Hall of Fame. The area's red dirt and rolling prairies also played a part in Oklahoma's famed Land Run of 1889.
- 100- and 50-mile options
- Red clay dirt can turn into a sticky, muddy mess.
- Course is marked, and GPX file is provided.
- Drop bag service for those without a support crew
- Finish line hug from promoter Bobby Wintle

ESSENTIAL GEAR

- Mud scraper and, if the course is wet, narrower than normal tires to increase mud clearance
- Spare derailleur hanger in case of drivetrain catastrophe

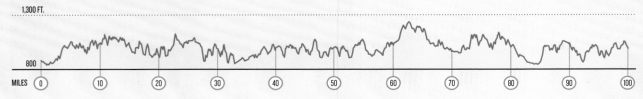

The red clay roads around Stillwater, Oklahoma, give venue to extraordinary cycling exploits. They also routinely ruin entire drivetrains.

Bobby Wintle addresses the anxious field before the start of the Land Run 100 (right). Finisher patches await tired cyclists (below). No one said gravel racing was easy, especially in Oklahoma (bottom).

One of Land Run's rugged sections leads
to a creek crossing and even more mud (left).
Every finisher receives a patch and a hearty
Wintle hug (top). Like all gravel events,
Land Run is a family affair (above).

Bobby Wintle
Land Run promoter

"Your bicycle must be in good working condition, with no parts needing replacement when stepping up to the start line. Take it to your local bike shop. Tell them about your event. Bring them a six-pack of their favorite beer or soda. Watch magic happen."

SPARES: "Extra tube, multi-tool, chain breaker. Most important for races like ours with possible mud is an extra derailleur hanger for your bike. Each bike is designed differently and has a specific hanger. Do some research with your local bike shop and make sure you get the right one. Next is knowing how to use a chain breaker and how to install the hanger on your bike properly. Talk with your mechanic. They would be stoked to help you learn this necessary repair."

"Cleaning brush or paint stir stick. Mud tends to stick to your bike. Something we saw at the start line of LRIOO were the front-runners taking shortened paint stir sticks and sliding them up into the leg opening of their bib shorts. Smart and effective for removing mud quickly from the drivetrain and tires. Having a Park Tool cog brush or a paint stir stick could help you finish instead of not finishing."

NUTRITION: "Water and enough of it. Know how your body reacts to different temperatures and in different course situations. The course changes each year, and if there is a lot of climbing you may end up drinking more water. Have plenty of water. Know when and where and how you are going to refill that water. Also, try to eat as much real food as possible. All of the nutritional supplements out there are great, but I tend to find that my body and mind are much more focused when I put real food in it. Make small burritos to take with you on the bike. I eat tons of Justin's Almond Butter in individual packets on rides. It's delicious, and I know it works for me. Try some things out before race day, and try not to switch up everything the day of the race."

Land Run promoter and enthusiastic fan, Bobby Wintle, cheers mid-race.

Austin Morris
2016 Land Run winner

BIKE: "I ride a Felt FIX cross bike. It offers more tire clearance than a road bike. You want a bike that can handle up to a 40mm tire, not necessarily because you are going to ride that big of a tire, but the space will provide more mud clearance. If I anticipate mud (which is almost always the case), I actually drop the tire size I run to a 32mm so it will not clog up as badly."

GEARING: "I use 50/34 chainrings and an 11–32 rear cassette. It is nice to have 30–32 teeth in the rear on some of the extended climbs."

TIRES: "I run the Panaracer GravelKings in 32mm or 35mm. They are light, roll fast, and still offer good, flat protection."

PEDALS: "If there is any chance of mud, I run Eggbeater mountain bike pedals with mountain bike shoes. They will clip in better than any other pedal when your shoe is covered in mud. Also, make sure the shoe is comfortable enough to run/walk in for a few miles."

EXTRAS: "I put a couple paint stirrers in my jersey. They work great for removing mud from the frame/fork so the tires will roll."

NUTRITION: "The time spent on the course dictates what type of food I eat. I think that the longer you are going to be out there, the more 'real' food you should bring. I always pack margarita Shot Bloks (two times the sodium to avoid cramps), gels, maybe a squeeze bottle of honey,

Austin Morris crosses a creek with Jay Petervary close behind.

and whatever liquid that will not make your stomach hurt when you are on the verge of overheating."

"Definitely cover yourself with sunscreen; it will probably be cool in the morning, but the sun will still drain your energy."

"The Land Run can be two completely different races. If the course is dry, it will be a fast 100-mile sprint. If it is muddy, it can be a test like no other, carrying the bike, removing mud from the frame just to get the tires to roll, just awesome."

Barry-Roubaix

Hastings, Michigan | April

The 3,200 racers and 2,000 spectators who attended Barry-Roubaix in 2016 made it the largest gravel race in the United States. Always the third Saturday in April, this Michigan event offers three distances, all relatively short, making them great for first-time gravel racers. With good course marking and corner marshals, navigation is made easy, allowing racers to focus on their efforts. It is certainly a race, with strong road and cyclocross competitors toeing the line. But like most gravel events, the atmosphere is welcoming. Race organizer Rick Plite happily shares that he "promotes an event, not just a race. All of my events have a grassroots feel to them, with handmade awards and beer afterwards. People like to chat and party a bit after a big ride."

Note that in his advice on page 39, Rick is aiming his comments at new riders. On the other hand, the 2015 women's elite champion, Mackenzie Woodring, gives tips on trying to win the event. Pick out the information that suits you best.

DEFINING FEATURES

- Hastings is a small town of just over 7,000 residents. The race is named for Barry County, an area southeast of Grand Rapids and west of Lansing, of which Hastings is the county seat.
- 62-, 36-, and 22-mile race distances offered
- Excellent course marking, corner marshals, GPX file, and cue sheet available
- Largest gravel race in the United States

ESSENTIAL GEAR

- Warm clothes; April weather in Michigan can be unpredictable
- Fast-rolling tires

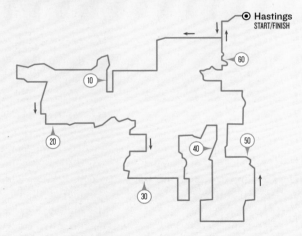

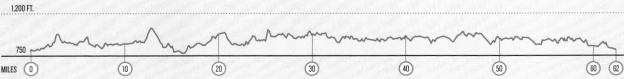

Barry-Roubaix can often be a wet, chilly race thanks to its early season timing.

The largest gravel race in the U.S. requires a lot of organizational work on the part of Rick Plite and his many volunteers.

Common at all gravel races is a wide range of riders and bikes (right). Barry-Roubaix is especially diverse.

Barry-Roubaix serves up gravel and hills. Even the 22-mile course has over 1,000 feet of climbing (above left). Sager Road is a technical two-track that spreads out the pack (left). Bar Mitts help keep hands toasty during spring conditions in Michigan (above).

Some take the racing more seriously than others, but all enjoy the festivities after the racing is done. Plite works hard to ensure that Barry-Roubaix is fun for the entire family and mindful of its community.

Rick Plite

Barry-Roubaix
promoter

Mackenzie Woodring

2015 Barry-Roubaix
women's elite champion

Mackenzie Woodring closes the book on another Barry-Roubaix.

"We tell people who are truly beginners to make sure to sign up for the proper distance. Don't ride to win, ride to finish. Enjoy it. Stop and take a photo. Don't go out and buy any special equipment. Ride what you have. At Barry-Roubaix, a road bike or 26-inch mountain bike will work."

BIKE: "I recommend a cyclocross bike for Barry-Roubaix with I×II gearing. Barry-Roubaix has 5,000 feet of climbing, so you're constantly changing gears, and I see dropped chains as a result of shifting between the big and small rings. My gearing of choice is a 36-tooth ring with an II–28 cassette, which is perfect for a 20 mile per hour average."

TIRES: "I'm a fan of Clement file tread tubular tires, as they have an aggressive knob on the outside for cornering. I've had no issues with flats with this tire, but I do carry a Vittoria Pit Stop just in case."

PREPARATION: "The best preparation is to actually ride the course. It's hard to mimic the Barry-Roubaix terrain in training, as the course is truly unique."

"The race selection happens within the first five minutes of the race. The race begins on pavement, where you jockey for position as you approach the first gravel section. As soon as the peloton hits the gravel, it rolls over 'The Three Sisters,' an affectionately known group of three climbs where the selection is made. You need a good warm-up and need to be ready to go anaerobic to stay with the lead group. Sager Road, approximately 30 minutes into the race, is another opportunity for selection to occur, as it is the only two-track section offered on the course. Staying in a group is key for a successful Barry-Roubaix!"

Trans Iowa

Grinnell, Iowa | April

This 330-plus-mile event is not for beginners. Competitors have 34 hours to complete the race, using only gas stations along the route for resupply. At times, riders will have to carry enough food and water to tackle over 100 miles of Iowa gravel. A new course each year ensures that riders will encounter a few surprises. With its early place on the gravel race calendar in April, temperatures can plummet during the race's nighttime hours. Conversely, daytime temperatures can climb high, making it tough on racers.

    The spring timing also requires a strong winter of training to ready one's mind and body for the rigors of riding for more than a day without significant stops. Racers will also need good lights and navigational skill practice during nighttime riding conditions.

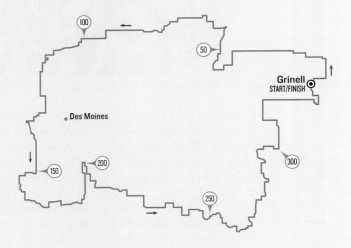

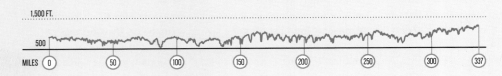

DEFINING FEATURES

- Grinnell is home to Grinnell College, where in 1889 the first football game west of the Mississippi River took place. The city was also a stopping point along the Mormon Pioneer Trail in the second half of the 19th century. It was also part of the Underground Railroad, a secret network of routes and safe houses that helped bring African slaves north to freedom in the 19th century.
- 300-plus miles of fast, somewhat smooth gravel
- Only recommended for seasoned ultradistance gravel racers
- No support crew; resupply via convenience stores
- Cue sheet navigation

ESSENTIAL GEAR

- Good lighting system and enough battery life to make it through the opening hours and an entire night of riding
- Well-practiced cue sheet navigation system
- Ability to carry sufficient fluids, food, and clothing

Enormous amounts of work, both from racers and Mark "Guitar Ted" Stevenson, prepare the Trans Iowa for its pre-dawn start.

Fast when dry, slow when wet, the gravel roads of Iowa are never easy. Tackling 330 miles of them takes years of training and months of preparation. Trans Iowa is not for beginners.

A word to the wise: If you see tracks like these, walk (above left). Good lighting can make or break you during the 330-mile Trans Iowa (left). Navigation is not always straightforward (above).

One of the steeper roads that Stevenson includes in Trans Iowa.

**Mark Stevenson,
a.k.a. Guitar Ted**

Trans Iowa promoter

Greg Gleason

2014, 2015, and 2016

Trans Iowa winner

"Lightweight, packable gear for rain or cold weather is essential. Wet weather and temperatures hovering down to near the freezing mark at night are not uncommon for Trans Iowa. Specialty gear like mud scrapers, which are often homemade by the riders, are great time savers after a muddy stretch of Level B Road. Cue sheet holders are another thing that falls under this category."

"Things have transitioned. When I first did it, I had no clue that I would win it. I got into it to simulate riding all day and all night with the Great Divide in mind. So my lighting the first year was a Light and Motion Stella and a Princeton Tec eight-battery unit. Because I wanted more light, I turned them both on. I carried spare batteries in my bag. This year, I have a dynamo hub and a kLite from Australia. It was amazing. The first year, I overpacked. Lots of extras. I packed everything and the kitchen sink. Last year I packed so light. I learned a lot in the past years because I commuted outside all year long, living in South Dakota. You learn tolerances. How cold is too cold? I learned how cold I could ride with just one jacket. An hour before the start, I'm checking the weather and doing a final pack."

"For gearing on a gravel cross bike, I like compact road gearing, 50/34 chainrings. I like 2×11 gearing. I have fallen in love with Shimano's electronic Di2 shifting. It's bulletproof. It shifts flawlessly. It's perfect for gravel. You name the condition, it works. I'm a big gear guy. As a time trial and road rider, I'm very comfortable with bigger gears. I don't pay much attention to my cassette. I think it's an 11–23. A lot of people will go with easier gears. There are a lot of hills, but they're rollers. Nothing too long."

"I prefer tubeless tires. Up to this point, I ran the Clement

USH. They're the most reliable tire on the planet, but they're tubed. In the future, I'll be on tubeless. I have some WTB Riddlers that I'm excited to try."

"The first year I went to the Trans Iowa clinic in Des Moines. Mike Johnson and Steve Fuller recommended carrying a bladder in a frame bag. So that's what I did the first year. The next year I put a CamelBak on because there was mud in the forecast. It keeps the bike lighter and easier to handle and carry. I don't have a problem with the weight on me instead of the bike."

"This year I didn't do any frame bags. I used a Revelate Pika seat pack, the lighter one. It's light but gives a little extra storage. I was able to carry everything I needed in it. For food, I used a Revelate Gas Tank, and I like to use Mountain Feedbags on each

side of my stem. Depending on the race, I'll use one of those for a bottle and the other for storage. At Trans Iowa, you know you'll want to start with clear glasses and switch to dark glasses and back. It's nice to have that extra storage in a handy position."

"For training, usually I do centuries. You don't need to do much more than that. It comes down to volume, really. You want to build each

month. Ideally, you start a year before the event so you can build gradually. So I try to do as many centuries as possible without killing myself. Just ride your bike as much as you can. It's important to go through the winter, not only from the endurance perspective but also to figure out the gear you need to carry. Stress it every now and then. It's good to try a ride without quite enough gear. You'll be surprised."

Cooperation can help the long miles seem a bit shorter.

Almanzo

Spring Valley, Minnesota | May

In terms of establishing the culture of gravel racing, many point to Chris Skogen's efforts with the Almanzo 100 in Minnesota. Beginning in 2007, the event was characterized by inclusivity and a welcoming feel. In the early years, Skogen handwrote welcome notes to each of the 400 riders who attended. The event, now organized by Spring Valley Tourism and Penn Cycle and Fitness, includes 100-, 162-, and 380-mile options. All events are free; participants are simply required to mail in a postcard that serves as their entry. May weather can be beautiful and bright, but can also bring rain and chilly temperatures.

DEFINING FEATURES

- Almanzo Wilder, the husband of author Laura Ingalls Wilder, lived near Spring Valley, Minnesota, before moving to South Dakota. The race is named for him. Spring Valley was also the home of Richard Sears of Sears, Roebuck and Company.
- 100-, 162-, and a multiday 380-mile courses on offer
- Mid-May Minnesota weather is a wild card
- GPX and cue sheet offered

ESSENTIAL GEAR

- Fast-rolling tires
- Good rain gear
- Appropriate spares: tubes, pump, chain tool, derailleur hanger

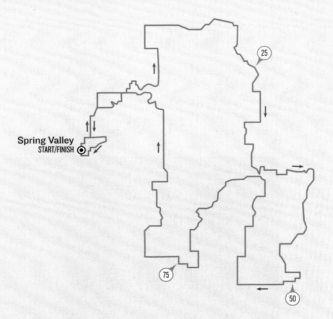

Spring Valley
START/FINISH

1,400 FT.

950

MILES 0   25   50   75   100

An unusual road hazard doesn't seem to faze Almanzo participants in Minnesota.

The rolling hills around Spring Valley, Minnesota, string out the hardy racers. As a free event, Almanzo draws in many first-timers and keeps veterans coming back.

Like all gravel events, Almanzo allows you to choose your own adventure, riding solo or sticking with other cyclists to share the fun and camaraderie.

The Almanzo gives you every opportunity to explore your limits.

Chris Skogen

Almanzo founder

Adam Bergman

2016 Almanzo 100 winner

"Check your ego at the door and other cliché entrance remarks. Don't haul ass downhill into a corner. Be smart and pick your lines right. Don't push it too hard or you'll end up picking rocks out of your elbow."

"Just ride your bike. That was the message I was trying to push the whole time. Just go out there and enjoy being present. Put one pedal over the other and just be here. Take in the sights and sounds that you're going to get on a dirt road. Everything is so much quieter and greener."

"I'm all about efficiency. I ride 8 to 10 hours a week, so the best thing I can do is be as efficient in bike/clothing equipment as possible to stay with the leaders. My choices really sound silly and triathlon-like dorky, but the difference over 100 miles between a 16 mph and a 17 mph average is close to 22 minutes. All the little choices add up."

TIRES: "Fastest rolling possible. I have only run slicks. I've found 35–38mm work the best around here. My tire brand of choice is Compass. Their weights in the bigger sizes are on par with high-end 25mm tires. No other brand sells the exact same tire from

26mm to 38mm and even bigger in 650b and 26-inch. I do not believe side knobs give any advantage to cornering in loose gravel, and [they] really hurt aerodynamics and rolling resistance. For racing, I use latex tubes and switch back to butyl tubes for commuting. I haven't gone tubeless in a while, mainly due to the hassle and the mess when they do flat. I've never ridden on flint rock gravel, so I would have to rethink tires and a tubeless setup for a Kanza-style event."

GEARING: "I used to run a 53/39 with an 11–32 cassette. That was a great setup. Shimano 10-speed was and is so versatile because it is compatible with the XT 9-speed mountain bike rear derailleur. The 39 is a great gear for riding headwind flats, and if you can get the cassette big enough is still okay for climbing. Lately I am using SRAM Force I.

I've become a fan. A 48-tooth front ring and an 11–36 cassette gives a huge range, and with gravel being rough, I don't notice any big gear jumps. If I were to spin out that setup, I probably should be coasting."

"One equipment choice I would like to try would be a Cirrus Cycles BodyFloat suspension seatpost. I could see that being a big advantage in efficiency and reducing body pain. Other odd choices: I use a swim cap over my helmet for aerodynamics. Haven't been hot yet with the setup. I keep the back vents exposed. If I were to get hot, I can just take it off. For this year's Almanzo, I used a skinsuit. It worked out okay. If I go skinsuit again, it will have to have pockets in the back, though. Clip-on aerobars are a must. So dorky, but it has to be the biggest advantage, especially in exposed headwind

sections. Also, it is just really comfortable. This leads to a small compromise, as I use an aluminum bar for a more secure clamp for the clip-on. I'm sure I give up a little bit in vibration damping over a carbon bar."

NUTRITION: "I'm a true believer that self-support is self-support. I don't drag friends and family out to feed me along some lonely back road for a free event and a handmade trophy. Plus, if there are water stops, this is a great time to take advantage of lugging all that water and cruise straight through. Three liters on the back is much more efficient than using a frame bag, and the bike handles better. I do use packing tape to tape down the top of the hydro pack to cheat the wind. For hot events, I will freeze the bladder and drink from bottles first. The bottles have mix in them for the extra calories. For food, I get

it done early. Eat a lot in the days before the race and as many bars as possible on the first half of the event. After that, if I can get a gel down, I'm happy. Last advantage of a hydration pack is it really makes you drink more. Not only is it easier, but the more you drink, the lighter it gets."

STRATEGY: "Have fun suffering, finish, and finish safely. It is an art to figure out the best line down a straight, flat gravel road, but there are general rules. Sand is slower than gravel, gravel is slower than dirt, and sometimes the grass ditch is the fastest. It really can be that simple, until wind is involved. Know the route. Nobody is there to guide you. I use both a Garmin Edge 25 and also cue sheets. Tandems are your friend. If you find yourself in a group with a tandem, climb at their pace and jump on their wheel for the free ride down the other side back to the group."

Dirty Kanza

Emporia, Kansas | Late May or early June

The fine folks who organize this event in Emporia, Kansas, have created something special. Cycling has changed this small college town in the 11 years since the race's inception. Racers are welcomed by business marquees all over town, at the oil change spot, the grocery store, hotels, and restaurants. But it isn't the town amenities that draw the riders; it's the gravel.

Nestled in the Flint Hills, the area is home to some of the most beautiful and brutally rugged gravel roads in the United States. As the name implies, the rock under your tires is flint, the same material Native Americans used to make arrow- and spearheads. It's sharp and it's everywhere. Avoiding punctures is vitally important for all participants. This leads many to mount up heavier-than-usual tires.

The distances offered, 200- and 100-mile races and 50- and 20-mile fun rides, add to the difficulty of the roads. Midwest heat and humidity in late May and early June also play a factor.

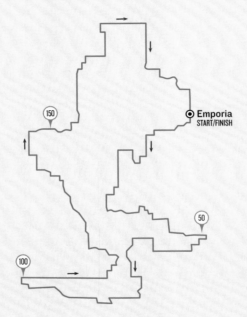

DEFINING FEATURES

- Emporia is the site of first observance of Veterans Day, in 1953. Emporia State University calls the city home and plays a significant role in the area's economy.
- 200-, 100-, 50-, and 20-mile options on sharp flint gravel
- Midwest heat and humidity possible
- Support crew required; crew can help only at checkpoints
- GPX, cue sheets, and maps offered; limited course marking

ESSENTIAL GEAR

- Puncture-resistant tires; tubeless is a good idea
- Gears low enough to tackle the loose gravel climbs

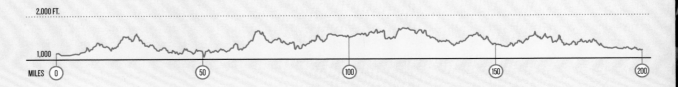

The beauty of the Flint Hills of Kansas is hard to miss, even if you don't have time to stop and smell the flowers.

Dirty Kanza starts in front of the historic Granada Theatre (above). A police escort leads the neutral rollout (above right). Early in the race, two lines of racers are common (below right).

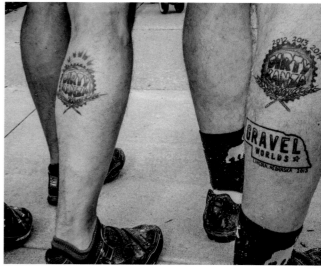

To ride or walk at creek
crossings? Your choice; you'll
get wet either way (left).
Gravel cycling isn't really a
cult (above); it just sometimes
seems that way.

The finish chute of Dirty Kanza awaits the arrival of the day's heroes. Any rider who crosses it is forever changed.

Jim Cummins

Dirty Kanza promoter

"Don't worry about what bike you have. Get out there and enjoy it. Get going. Enjoy the ride. Enjoy the experience. Go discover what you're capable of. Be ready to be surprised. You're going to find that you're capable of so much more than you thought you were. Gravel is going to give you the platform for that discovery."

Yuri Hauswald

2015 Dirty Kanza 200 winner

"I don't really care if you ride a mountain bike with skinnies or a cyclocross bike with fatties. All I care about is that you've spent a fair amount of time on whatever rig you're riding and that it fits *you*. I highly recommend getting a professional fit. If you are not comfortable on the bike, you're in for a very long day."

"My steed of choice for any gravel or mixed terrain event is the Marin Cortina Pro-A carbon disc brake cyclocross bike outfitted with Atom Composite wheels, a WTB Nano 40mm tire on the front

Yuri Hauswald trains both body and mind for the race.

and Riddler 37mm tubeless tire on the rear, and a WTB Silverado saddle. Two crucial contact points are the tires, and more importantly, your saddle. For the flinty, sharp gravel that you find at Dirty Kanza 200, I run as wide a tubeless tire as possible, with sturdy sidewalls and a relatively low tread profile that, hopefully, has some good side knobs for cornering."

Crusher in the Tushar

Beaver, Utah | July

Beaver, Utah, birthplace of outlaw train robber Butch Cassidy, plays home to the start of this climber's delight of a gravel race. Retired pro cyclist Burke Swindlehurst organizes the Crusher to showcase the beautiful roads of Utah's Tushar Mountains and Fishlake National Forest. With 10,000 feet of climbing in just 70 miles, you need to bring your A game to this event. Because of the climbing and fast descents, some competitors choose to race on mountain bikes, though top finishers are usually aboard cyclocross or gravel bikes.

DEFINING FEATURES

- Located in southwest Utah, Beaver was the home of Philo T. Farnsworth, inventor of devices that made television possible. The town of Beaver was the first in the state of Utah to be electrified, thanks to a hydroelectric plant on the Beaver River. The area was also part of the Mormon trade route from Salt Lake City to Los Angeles in the mid-19th century.
- Very hilly course that starts at 6,000 feet, with a 50/50 split of pavement and dirt
- Five aid stations stocked with provisions
- Course is very well marked; no need for cue sheet. GPX file provided

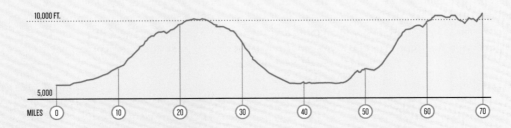

ESSENTIAL GEAR

- Low climbing gears are required, with many racers electing to use mountain bikes
- Good brakes for rough descents

Crusher in the Tushar is a climber's delight with 10,000 feet of climbing on dirt roads.

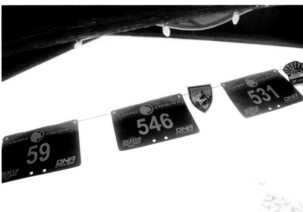

The Crusher is known for its tough competition and beautiful scenery. A group forms on one of the race's pavement sections (above).

The dappled light of an aspen alley gives respite from the summer heat (left). Burke Swindlehurst and his crew are ready with impromptu ponchos and massive amounts of refreshments (above).

The expo and bike parking areas at the Crusher are an indicator of the event's popularity. The large, speeding peloton is too.

Because of the steep climbing and fast dirt descents, many racers prefer a mountain bike. But others argue that a cyclocross or gravel bike is the way to go.

Burke Swindlehurst

Crusher in the Tushar
promoter

BIKE: "First year was 50/50 split with mountain bikes and 'cross bikes. Now it's more gravel bikes. Still 35 percent [of participants] are on mountain bikes. Ride whatever you feel most comfortable on. A mountain biker would be crazy to go out and buy a gravel bike thinking they'll go faster. The bikes handle totally differently. Personally, I love challenging myself on a 'cross bike. Sometimes I'm walking. But I'm amazed at how capable a 'cross bike is. It's so fun and people are stunned."

Tyler Wren

2011 Crusher in the Tushar
winner

BIKE: "The technical side of the Crusher is always really interesting for me. I was doing a lot of prototype testing for Jamis on the Renegade. It was a great course for me to give feedback. That type of adventure bike is perfect for a course like that. It has a lot of climbing. That's where the race is won. But at the same time, you can't afford to lose a lot of time on the descents. No matter what bike you have, you'll reach a point where you're on the wrong bike. I always thought that a 'cross bike or adventure bike was a good choice for me. I spent a lot of time on that type of bike, so I was really comfortable on it. Make sure it's a bike that's comfortable for a long ride but that you can also aggressively descend on. Even for the winner, it's a six-hour day. For others, it can be a ten-hour day."

TIRES: "I used a lot of different tires at that event. I found that something with a semi-slick tread with aggressive side knobs is great. You need something with good knobs for descending the Col de Crush. But the rest of the time, you want a tire that rolls really well."

BRAKES: "Braking power is really important too. The washboard switchbacks are tricky. I recommend disc brakes, hydraulic disc brakes if you can get them."

Gravel Worlds

Lincoln, Nebraska | August

Created as a tongue-in-cheek swipe at the Union Cycliste Internationale (UCI), the governing body of professional cycling, winners receive a bright pink jersey with rainbow stripes (the UCI world champion jerseys are white with rainbow bands). This 150-mile event in Lincoln, Nebraska, takes place during the heat of late August. With a smooth, sometimes sandy road surface, the going is fast except for the constant up and down of the Nebraska hills. Over the course of 150 miles, racers climb close to 12,000 feet as they loop the city of Lincoln. While the course and number of aid stations change each year, the event includes several required checkpoints and many oases hosted by friends of the promoters. Homemade pickles, cheese curds, tacos, Cokes, ice water, and fruit are all available at regular intervals—midwestern hospitality at its best.

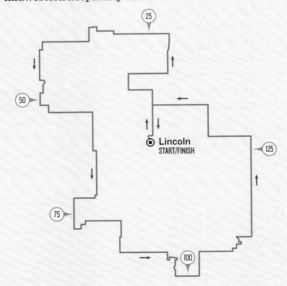

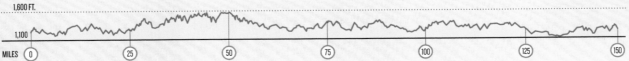

DEFINING FEATURES

- As the capitol of Nebraska, Lincoln is the state's political hub and the home of the University of Nebraska. The area surrounding Lincoln is laced by beautiful gravel roads that constantly climb and descend through agricultural fields and pastures.
- 150 miles of fast, rolling Nebraska gravel
- Late August heat and humidity
- GPX and cue sheet navigation; no course marking
- No support crew allowed; resupply at convenience stores and race checkpoints

ESSENTIAL GEAR

- Ability to carry sufficient water to combat the heat
- A sense of humor, as the Pirate Cycling League (the organizing club) keeps it light!

A group that includes Land Run promoter Bobby Wintle tops a Nebraska hill at Gravel Worlds.

A tandem team reaches for start line high fives, keeping the mood light (above). Neil Shirley and Brian Jensen, two former pro roadies, battled out the 2015 edition with Shirley taking the title (right).

Joe Stiller, in the blue and black kit (left), races in the fat bike category at events all over the country, even racing the Iditarod Trail Invitational in Alaska. The smooth gravel in Nebraska means higher speeds and larger groups drafting one another (above).

In 2015 Tim and Kristi Mohn, co-owners of Dirty Kanza with Jim Cummins and LeLan Dains, raced their tandem to a Gravel Worlds title.

Corey Godfrey

Gravel Worlds founder

BIKES/GEARING: "Run what ya brung! We see so many different bikes and setups at Gravel Worlds. 'Cross, road, mountain, touring, fatbikes, cargo bikes, hybrids, commuters, old-school cruisers. It's fun to see all different bikes. As far as gearing, 'cross bikes with 1×11 or 2×10 with compact road or 'cross gearing are common if you wanna go fast. The hills are plentiful at Gravel Worlds, but are relatively short and punchy. A road bike with compact gearing would also be an option. For single speeds, I personally prefer 42×18, but anything would work as long as you stay on top of it."

TIRES: "The gravel/dirt around Lincoln is relatively tame compared to some other surrounding states in the Midwest. For 'cross bikes, a 35mm tire should work fine; 25 or 28mm tires on a road bike and 2.0 inches on a mountain bike work too. I prefer a file tread or a semi-slick. Punctures aren't common, but tubeless is still prudent."

NUTRITION: "We try to keep the resupply options plentiful in Gravel Worlds. Fifty miles is the longest in between resupply stops. I would recommend at least three bottles and a thousand calories in between resupplies."

STRATEGY: "Don't burn all your matches in the first few hours. Settle in for an all-day pace and stay on top of your hydration and nutrition early. Make sure you navigate yourself, and don't just follow the person the front of you."

Neil Shirley

2015 Gravel Worlds champion

"There's only one market, where you have to stop and buy a Powerball ticket [this changes each year]. There were also three neutral checkpoints with snacks and water, all in the 50-mile range. I ran three bottles in 2015. It was quite hot and windy. You'd go into a block headwind for 45 minutes and think, 'This sucks.' Then you'd turn, get a crosswind, and it was great. Then you'd turn again and ride with a tailwind, and you'd overheat in five minutes, dying for a headwind again."

"The roads are proper gravel roads. Maintained gravel roads. What you'll find is varied gravel. You'll come across some roads with fresh-laid gravel, and that makes it quite technical. There is no line. But there aren't many sections like that. Usually there are three good lines because of the cars. They're fast roads. Expect 2 miles per hour average faster than at Dirty Kanza. I ran a 32mm wide tire last year with minimal tread, and it was plenty. It has also been won on a Trek Domane with 28mm tires."

"The one thing that really surprised me was all the climbing. It all comes in short climbs, but they're nonstop, and often with a headwind. I had 11,000 feet of climbing over 150 miles in 2015."

Deerfield Dirt Road Randonnée

Deerfield, Massachusetts | August

Winding its way through the hills of western Massachusetts, this event—fondly known as D2R2—is a perfect first taste of the best that dirt roads have to offer. The day includes a strong culinary aspect, with breakfast, lunch, and dinner offered, as well as stocked checkpoints. There are several distances available, so choose the ride that suits you best. But note that the area is home to many steep grades. If you're in doubt, choose a distance one stop shorter than usual to ensure that you enjoy your day on the bike.

Riders can start whenever they like to explore the area's hills and lanes. Unlike the wide-open spaces of the Midwest and farther west, New England is dense with deciduous trees and beautiful foliage. Massachusetts can be quite hot in August, so take care to stay hydrated.

The event is a fundraiser for the Franklin Land Trust, an organization dedicated to the conservation of the region's land. So know that you're not only having a good time, you're doing it for a good cause.

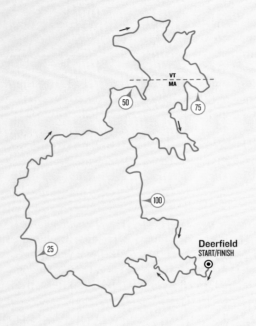

DEFINING FEATURES

- As the most northwestern outpost in the early territory of New England, the Deerfield area was the site of several violent encounters between settlers and Native Americans, as well as their French allies, in the late 17th and early 18th centuries. Located in western Massachusetts, Deerfield is due east of Albany, New York, and less than 20 miles from the Vermont and New Hampshire state borders to the north.
- Late August timing means hot temperatures
- Cue sheet navigation required
- Range of distances from 20 to 112 miles

ESSENTIAL GEAR

- Low gearing for the steep inclines
- Wide tires and spare tubes for the area's loose roads

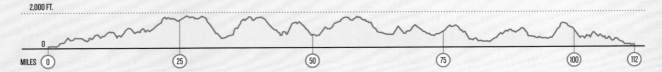

The leafy forests of Franklin County, Massachusetts, host the Deerfield Dirt Road Randonnée.

The noncompetitive nature of D2R2 encourages riders to take in the landscapes as they pedal through. Sunflowers, covered bridges and high-quality dirt roads ensure a pleasant day.

The winding roads and constant hills of northwestern Massachusetts challenge riders of all abilities. Different distances allow you to tailor your experience.

D2R2 raises money for the Franklin Land Trust, a local land conservation organization.

Matt Roy

*Multiple Deerfield Dirt Road
Randonnée (D2R2) participant,
Green Mountain Double Century
record holder*

GEARING: "There are multiple sections with grades over 20 percent along the route, and traction is critical. The more you can stay seated, the better your chance at getting up the toughest climbs, particularly on the super-loose sandy sections. I've done it in the past with 34×28 as my easy gear, but I've gotten smarter since then. The closer you can get to I:I, the happier you'll be!"

TIRES: "Tire choice is highly dependent on the conditions of the roads. After a dry summer, the roads will be loose and pretty chewed up,

so the bigger the better. I've done it with as narrow as a 28mm tire, but again, I've gotten smarter since then. I'll be rolling a 40mm tire this year. The roads are often graded with fresh stones when you least expect it, so plan on encountering golf ball–sized stones, and bring extra tubes!"

NUTRITION: "It gets *hot* in August in western Massachusetts. As tempting as the pre-ride beers are the night before, I highly recommend pre-hydrating. I try to put down at least 64 ounces of drink mix the day before the event. Weather will play a part on day of, but it's a well-run event, with breakfast, lunch, and dinner provided and options for water along the way. On hot days, it's easy to lose your appetite, so bring along a little something that you find yourself craving on your longer rides. Personally, I like

Matt Roy rides rain or shine, day or night during his endurance events.

Little Debbie Oatmeal Pies. These things are horrible for you, but when you need calories, *bam*: 75 cents. One of these has gotten me out of a jam more than once!"

"D2R2 is a fun event, so let it be fun. To really enjoy it, don't let D2R2 be the first day you

spend on a gravel road. It's good to get the miles in, but if you're anxious about taking a corner at 30-plus miles per hour on tires you've only ridden twice, you might be missing out on the best of D2R2."

Rebecca's Private Idaho

Ketchum, Idaho | September

Legendary endurance athlete Rebecca Rusch became smitten with gravel racing after taking part in the Dirty Kanza. Rusch saw an opportunity for a gravel event in her own backyard. Timed for the beginning of fall weather in early September, temperatures can be chilly at altitude. But the payoff is incredible alpine views and great roads in a remote basin above Ketchum. Despite strong roots in mountain biking, Rusch loves the inclusive nature of gravel riding. "It's a little technical for mountain bikers, and it's exciting for road riders too. It still requires concentration. You have to pay attention. Elite racers can come, and total beginners can come, and both will have a good time. I want elites and beginners to feel welcome. We have a junior category. I want RPI to be really inclusive. We have a party, a parade, and a festival after the race. It's a complete weekend in Idaho for racers and their families."

DEFINING FEATURES

- Ketchum neighbors the ski resort town of Sun Valley. The area was born during the mining boom in the late 19th century. It was the home of Ernest Hemingway, a lover of the area's hunting and fishing until his suicide in his Warm Springs home near Ketchum.
- 94-mile Big Potato and 56-mile Small Fry distances are well marked
- Racing at altitude, starting at 6,000 feet in Ketchum
- Opening climb up Trail Creek Road separates the pack quickly

ESSENTIAL GEAR

- Low gears to cope with climbing at altitude
- Warm layers for a potentially cold start to the day

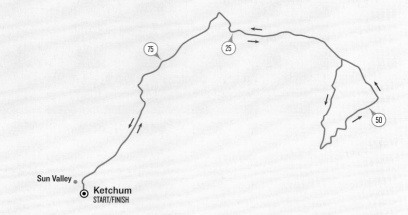

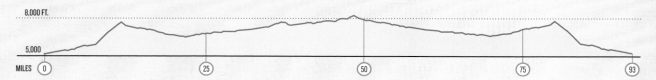

Rebecca's Private Idaho takes in remote dirt roads in the Sawtooth National Forest outside of Ketchum.

Rusch rides portions of the day patrolling for riders in distress and greeting old friends (above). Aid stations include roasted potatoes, a local crop, at RPI (right). The day's opening climb isn't easy, but it's also the day's final descent (opposite).

Much of the RPI route is exposed, making cooperation important (left).
After-race festivities include live music and gelande quaffing, a drinking game
that involves sliding a glass of beer across a long table to a teammate (above).

Rebecca Rusch

*Rebecca's Private Idaho
(RPI) promoter*

STRATEGY: "The biggest hill is right at the beginning. So if you can make it to the top at mile 10, you're in good shape. It's a lollipop course. The 50-mile is an out and back. So if you aren't sure you can finish, you can always turn around. It's really approachable."

EQUIPMENT: "We've had past winners on mountain bikes and skinny road bike tires. Around 70 percent of participants are on gravel bikes. For comfort, if you're not used to being in the saddle that long, a hardtail 29er is great. Think long and

Rebecca Rusch has won the Leadville 100 on four occasions.

hard about your tire choice. If you're a roadie, try to get a 40mm tire. If you're on a mountain bike, you can go down to a skinnier, fast-rolling tire. Don't get hung up on equipment, though.

Most important is to be comfortable. The opening climb is also the final descent, with no guardrail and a big drop. You need to be confident in your bike. Bring spares so you can fix a flat."

Meredith Miller

2012 RPI winner

TIRES: "Clement's MSO 36 is a perfect race tire for RPI."

GEARING: "A double chainring with 50/34 gearing and an 11–32 cassette is good. You need small gears for the climb, but you need big gears for the fast, flat sections."

STRATEGY: "Do your due diligence in training on gravel roads. There is very little pavement, so you need to be super comfortable on dirt and gravel. Don't go too deep on the first climb. There's still a long, tough ride to go! Find a group that's your speed and try to stick with them. You'll make new friends, and the ride will be more enjoyable than riding alone."

Grinduro

Quincy, California | October

Borrowing its format from enduro mountain bike racing, where only sections of a prescribed course are timed, Grinduro is a new kid on the gravel block. But in its first year, the event garnered high praise from attendees. Many racers camped in the area and partied afterwards. A catered lunch mid-ride keeps racers fueled up. With pavement, dirt, and singletrack, bike choice is difficult. Gravel and cyclocross bikes are popular, but a cross-country mountain bike is just as at home.

This course shown here is from 2017.

DEFINING FEATURES

- Quincy is nestled in the Sierra Nevada mountains and is a small gold rush town founded in 1858.
- Timed sections mean that strategy comes into play in new ways.
- Marked course has a catered lunch stop.
- Early October date makes it great for cyclocross racers looking for a break from barriers and an attractive end-of-season race for gravel aficionados.

ESSENTIAL GEAR

- While the course changes from year to year, many argue that a light mountain bike may be faster than a gravel or 'cross bike.
- With its mountainous terrain, you'll want low gears and good brakes.

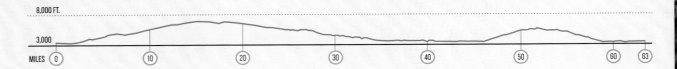

Singletrack sections of Grinduro allow riders aboard mountain bikes to shine.

Because only designated sections are timed, the riding in between is relaxed and social (left). Flats happen; carry spares (above). Most competitors camp near the start/finish, adding to the low-key vibe (right).

A mix of highly skilled lounging, nutritious mid-ride food, and stellar roads are all part of the Grinduro experience.

Live music right in the middle of the campground keeps the party rolling long after wheels have stopped turning. Plenty of frosty beers are hoisted as well. Everything benefits the Sierra Buttes Trail Stewardship.

Heading through the woods for another spectacular day of racing.

Barry Wicks

2015 Grinduro winner

GEARING: "Use one or many, depending on your preference. I think I saw at least one guy on a fixie, and he seemed to be having an awesome time. I used normal gears and won, but that's not why I won."

TIRES: "Pick ones that will keep air in them. It's not as easy as it sounds."

NUTRITION: "I like eating pickles and beef jerky, but luckily at Grinduro they give you pretty much all the food you need at the aid stations and lunch stop. Plus there was beer at the bottom of the last stage, so that was clutch. I did almost puke after lunch because we went straight into an hour-long sustained 15 percent climb, but everyone is in the same boat, so chow down."

STRATEGY: "My strategy was to spaz out as hard as I could on the first two stages. Then I picked a good group for the pavement section and mostly just motivated everyone to go hard in the paceline. On the last stage, I had multiple near-death experiences, but I had lowered my seat a couple of inches and had been doing my push-ups, so I survived and did a sweet skid across the finish line right up to the beer cooler. That's probably why I won, but I didn't even know I had won for a while after that, so it's unclear."

Barry Wicks made his bones as a mountain bike and cyclocross pro.

The *wanderwegs* of Germany host Gravel Fondo, a race in the Black Forest.

④ ONE-DAY INTERNATIONAL EVENTS

Gravel racing is by no means a strictly American endeavor. Mixed-surface riding is gaining popularity worldwide. Although the collection of events in this chapter is not comprehensive, it does represent an interesting sampling of the gravel events you'll find multiplying around the globe.

The same rules of preparation outlined in Chapter 2 apply to international races. However, you will want to make your plans further in advance. You need to make sure your passport is current and is good for at least six months beyond your date of arrival, that you have a visa if you need one, and that your travel arrangements include a solid plan for getting your bike and gear safely to the starting line. It's wise to be sure that your inoculations are up to date as well.

Arriving at least a week ahead of the race will help minimize jet-lag issues and will also help you adapt to a new language, new food, and a new culture. Getting in a few good rides before the race itself will spin the airline cramps out of your legs and give you a chance to explore your new surroundings. Those rides will also help you sort out the travel issues with your bike that inevitably arise, and having a few free days ahead of the race will give you time to track down whatever spare parts you may need.

Great Otway Gravel Grind

Forrest, Victoria, Australia | February

If you are determined to ride gravel year-round, head down under. The Great Otway Gravel Grind (GOGG) is held alongside the Otway Odyssey mountain bike event, a renowned Australian gathering with over 1,200 participants. Whether you want to put your head down and race one of the two distances or prefer to take your time and regroup with friends periodically, GOGG has provisions for both. The area's magnificent landscapes are an almost untouched wilderness bisected by smooth dirt tracks perfect for a day in the saddle. Large tree ferns and the Otway rain forest offer a stark contrast to the settings of midwestern events in the United States.

DEFINING FEATURES

- 97- and 49-kilometer options (60 miles and 30 miles) on smooth dirt roads
- Midcourse time-outs pause the race clock so you can regroup with friends or only race one-half of the course.
- Long course includes a stretch along the Great Ocean Road.
- A food festival plays host to the start and finish.

TRAVEL TIPS

- The town of Forrest is quite small, with only 200 residents, but has a bike shop/café.
- Accommodation in a range of bed-and-breakfasts near Forrest or camp in the RV park. A 40-minute drive to Apollo Bay offers beachside hotels.
- The closest international airport is Tullamarine (Melbourne), a two-hour drive.

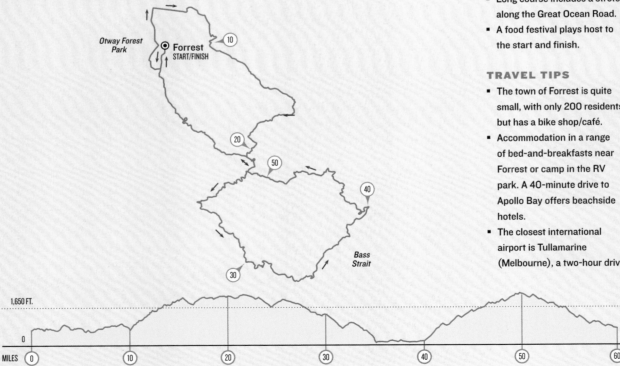

Otway Forest Park

Forrest
START/FINISH

Bass Strait

1,650 FT.

0

MILES   0   10   20   30   40   50   60

Views of the Bass Strait, the piece of ocean that separates mainland Australia and Tasmania, don't disappoint.

Among the most beautiful routes in the world, the Great Ocean Road is one of the highlights on the Big Ring course (right). Rollout for the Great Otway Gravel Grind takes place on pavement. Quickly, though, you find your way to the lovely dirt and gravel roads of Victoria's coastal region (above).

The roads used in the Great Otway Gravel Grind are engineered for two-wheel-drive cars, meaning they're fairly smooth. Tires at least 32mm wide are recommended but mountain bikes are also appropriate. Café stops are encouraged.

Ridden solo or with a group, the Great Otway Gravel
Grind is an amazing way to experience Australia.

Ali Deane

*Marketing and communications
manager for Rapid Ascent,
the GOGG organizer*

"This is an event that's designed for all riders on all types of bikes, ridden most comfortably on a gravel grinder or cyclocross bike. It can easily be completed on a road bike, the thicker your tires the better."

Sam Maffett

*General manager
of Rapid Ascent,
the event organizer*

"The roads are not overly rough nor technical nor muddy. So narrower tires are okay, and riders could complete it on almost any bike."

"A skinny road tire would make for a rough ride, so a wider tire on a road or cyclocross bike would be perfect."

"While the course is hilly, with a fair amount of ascending, there are no walls to climb up with super-steep roads. Standard gearing would suffice. Something like a 42-tooth chainring and an 11–32 cassette would work fine."

"A unique aspect of the event is a time-out stop in the middle of the courses. The long course time-out is located on the Great Ocean Road, where you can find cafés in the villages of Kennett River and Wye River. This allows riders to grab a coffee and cake, wait for friends, and relax a little. Riders can refuel then and there. The short course is similar, with a time-out on the course near the midway point. This will have a couple coffee vans and some fruitcake and lollies to top up on. Otherwise, riders can carry whatever nutrition they prefer, so long as they don't drop the wrappers!"

La Gravel66

Pyrénées-Orientales, France | March

Organized by bicycle maker Caminade, La Gravel66 is part of a series of gravel events around France. Close to Perpignan in the south of France near the Spanish border, this ride explores the quiet dirt and gravel tracks where Caminade developed its gravel bike. La Gravel66 is a spirited group ride with a focus on levity and six timed segments, similar in format to Grinduro. Expect fun and post-ride beers.

While the event is small, event organizer Sylvain Renouf says that interest for future editions is high, as gravel riding in the Pyrénées-Orientales is among the best in France. Difficulty is also high, but the beauty of the landscape more than makes up for the struggles. While the mileage may seem low at around 52 miles, with over 6,000 feet of climbing, riders can expect to be on their bikes for over four hours.

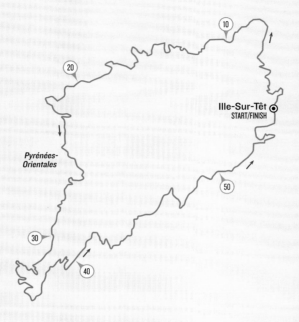

DEFINING FEATURES

- Unsupported on loose and chunky gravel roads in the south of France
- 45–50-mile distance, with a new course each year

TRAVEL TIPS

- Fly into Perpignan, France, or Girona or Barcelona, Spain.
- Camping spots and hotels are plentiful in the area.
- "Come with a good bike to enjoy the ride, and bring some beers!" —Sylvain Renouf

With the Pyrénées as a backdrop, **La Gravel66** is a fun, low-key gravel event in a gorgeous location.

Sylvain Renouf, La Gravel66's organizer, rates the gravel roads in the Pyrénées-Orientales department as the best in France. While currently a small event, interest is high and La Gravel66 is expected to grow each year.

Timed segments keep the riding lively, but in between the group regroups and rolls *ensemble*. Like all gravel events, punctures can be expected. Be sure to carry spares.

Roads in the Pyrénées-Orientales can be rugged. Low gearing and tires 38mm or larger are recommended.

The riding and the views reward the effort of getting there.

Sylvain Renouf
Organizer of the La Gravel66

BIKE: "We recommend a bike like our Caminade gravel bike, with a comfortable frame (steel is perfect), disc brakes, tires around 38mm and tubeless, and gravel geometry that is stable but high performance."

TIRES: "Our favorite tire model is the all-new Hutchinson Override. These come in 700×35 or 700×38 in tubeless. They are fast on the road and with a good grip and volume for dirt roads and tracks with stones. Weight is really low at 350 grams per tire, and you can use low pressures, around three bar (43.5 psi)."

GEARING: "We like 1×11. It's easy to use, reliable, light, and quiet. You are always sure to use the right gear as quickly as possible. An 11–36 cassette with a 38-tooth chainring is enough to ride everything. You can also go for a 10–42 cassette and a 42-tooth chainring if you are building a road bike/gravel bike. We use SRAM Force and Rival groups."

NUTRITION: "Our events are unsupported, so every rider should bring enough food. For water, there are sources in every village or at trailheads close to the forest. It is not an issue. At the finish, everyone brings some beer and food, and we do a sort of party. It's a lot of fun."

Dirty Reiver

Kielder Castle, United Kingdom | April

Located in the Borders area, the region along the English and Scottish line, is "a vast playground for long-distance riding," according to Paul Errington, the organizer of the Dirty Reiver. Despite the preconception that the British Isles are a crowded place, this area in northern England offers unexpected remoteness. Covering 124 miles of packed-gravel logging roads, this noncompetitive event still rewards fast riding by classifying finishers as "Highwaymen" if they finish in under 8 hours, 30 minutes and "Outlaws" if they finish in under 10 hours. "Brigands" are those who finish in more than 10 hours.

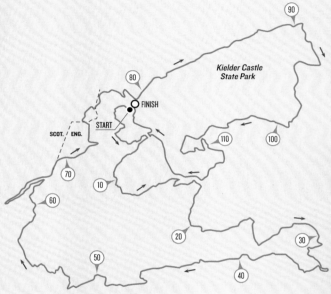

DEFINING FEATURES

- A 200-kilometer (124-mile) loop on packed gravel roads with long, steady climbs and fast descents, the course is rarely flat.
- GPX file provided and the use of a GPS is encouraged.
- Three stocked aid stations and a midpoint drop bag option are provided.
- Camping available

ESSENTIAL GEAR

- The event website has a helpful list of required gear, including an emergency whistle, survival blanket, waterproof jacket, front and rear lights, a mobile phone, a hat, ride food, and the ability to carry 1.5 liters of water.

TRAVEL TIPS

- Newcastle International Airport is the closest, though Glasgow is also an option.

The Dirty Reiver route takes in some fast dirt roads as well as many small, rugged tracks.

The stark beauty of the Borders area is hard to deny. At 1,500 feet, Blakehope Nick (above) is the highest point along the Kielder Forest Drive, one of the highest roads in the United Kingdom. As you may expect, the area's weather can be wet and chilly. A frost (left) is possible and it's a good idea to bring good rain gear, including a rear fender (below left).

The rolling green hills of
England dominate sections
of the Dirty Reiver. Tough riding
only seems to bring riders
together, a worldwide hallmark
of gravel riding and racing.

Paul Errington
Dirty Reiver promoter

BIKE: "The course really favors drop bar bikes with a decent size tire. That said, we won't discourage you riding any bike you are confident you can cover distance on."

TIRES: "Our recommendation is a 40c minimum width if your bike allows. Right now, the Panaracer GravelKing SK 40c seems to be a great tire for the event."

GEARING: "The climbs on the course are long, but the gradient is never extreme. A cyclocross chainset (46/36) with an 11–32 cassette gives plenty of options. A 1×11 setup is also an option. Just play with the gears so when you are tired you have something low enough for the climbs."

NUTRITION: "We expect riders to be carrying enough for their projected finish times. Time should be taken on training rides to refine needs and figure out what works and quantities. We have three feed stations along the route that offer a chance for topping up supplies. We also offer to take a drop bag to Feed 2 at the 100-kilometer mark."

Paul Errington takes part in gravel races all over the globe.

Pirinexus 360 Challenge

Girona, Catalonia, Spain | June

Covering a 350-kilometer (217-mile) loop of paved and gravel roads in the northern region of Catalonia, the Pirinexus 360 takes in gravel, dirt, and quiet paved roads near the cycling mecca of Girona, Spain. Organizer Jordi Cantal is preaching the gospel of gravel to anyone who will listen. With great weather, exceptional food, and close proximity to both the Mediterranean Sea and the Pyrénées mountains, Catalonia is something of a cycling paradise. Though it is one of the more affluent regions in Spain, a large network of dirt roads still crisscrosses the area to connect small villages and towns. The Pirinexus 360 Challenge hits many of the best gravel roads and takes in three mountain passes, a healthy dose of Catalan riding by anyone's standards.

DEFINING FEATURES

- A 350-kilometer loop of mixed-surface riding in Catalonia through the Pyrénées into France and back along the Costa Brava with a 20-hour time limit
- Not for beginners, but aimed at seasoned ultra-endurance cyclists

TRAVEL TIPS

- The Girona area offers good roads, great food, and excellent weather. June is usually dry and warm, but not hot.
- Barcelona is the nearest international airport. For inter-European travel, Barcelona Costa-Brava is also an option.

For those in search of a truly challenging mixed-surface event, the Pirinexus 360 will deliver.

The Pirinexus 360 is a unique way to discover the roads of Catalonia, both paved and dirt, in a single go. You'll need an adventurous spirit and some fitness to get it done, however.

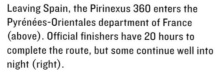

Leaving Spain, the Pirinexus 360 enters the Pyrénées-Orientales department of France (above). Official finishers have 20 hours to complete the route, but some continue well into night (right).

The village of Amer is reached early in the Pirinexus. Leaving here, the route heads north towards the Pyrénées and France.

Quiet double tracks are interspersed with small mountain paths.

Jordi Cantal
Pirinexus 360 Challenge
organizer

BIKE: "All bikes are allowed, although the most appropriate are gravel or cyclocross bikes. Road bikes with 28mm tires and mountain bikes with slicks are also used."

TIRES: "Your tires must be puncture resistant and smooth riding. I ride a cyclocross bike with Schwalbe Marathon Plus 32mm touring tires with tubes and additional protection to prevent punctures. Bigger tires will be more comfortable but also have more rolling resistance. Other popular models are Continental's Travel Contact and Panaracer's GravelKing."

GEARING: "I recommend the same as a road bike. An 11–28 cassette is sufficient, and compact chainrings, 52/36 or 50/34, are okay."

NUTRITION: "There are three food stations with sandwiches, pasta, fruit, cakes, energy bars and three stations with liquid refreshments like water and energy drinks."

STRATEGY: "Participants have 20 hours to complete the course. They leave Girona at sunrise, heading north, cross the Pyrénées, ride through a French village, and then cross back into Catalonia. Eventually, near sunset, they return to Girona. The route passes through all types of terrain, tarmac roads, many gravel tracks, and small urban zones. The landscape changes every kilometer."

La Resistance

Talloires, France | September

Situated in the Haute-Savoie region of France,
and starting and finishing on the shore of Lake Annecy,
La Resistance is a difficult day of riding on pavement
and gravel around a route that pays homage to the
French Resistance fighters of World War II. Two routes
of this noncompetitive event are offered, with 130- and
90-kilometer distances (80 and 55 miles). Both take in
La Route de la Soif, a high alpine gravel road with fantastic
views of Mont Blanc and beyond.

There is also a three-day bikepacking route, the Tour de
la Resistance, which covers 360 kilometers (224 miles) and
climbs nearly 30,000 feet. It's an unsupported way to take
in the area's beautiful scenery before riding the last day
supported alongside other La Resistance riders.

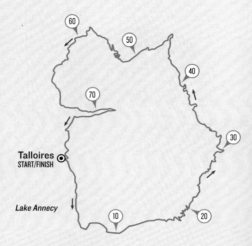

Talloires
START/FINISH

Lake Annecy

DEFINING FEATURES

- A mix of gravel and pavement;
  the significant climbs are
  paved to the Col de l'Arpettaz
  (15 kilometers [9 miles]
  at 8 percent grade, and rated
  hors catégorie), and Col de
  Glieres (7 kilometers [4 miles]
  at 10 percent grade, rated
  Category 2).

- The iconic alpine gravel road,
  La Route de la Soif, arrives
  after the opening climb and
  gives an unfettered view of
  Mont Blanc.
- Finish at La Guinguette, a
  large party with dancing, food,
  and drink where more than
  500 fete the night away.

TRAVEL TIPS

- Geneva airport is closest, and
  a 45-minute drive to Talloires.
- Accommodations run the
  gamut in Talloires, with
  everything from the five-star
  Abbaye de Talloires to two-
  and three-star hotels and four
  campgrounds. Book early.

6,000 FT.

750

MILES 0   10   20   30   40   50   60   70   80

The beautiful setting where cyclists now gather was also the site of one of the French underground's last stands during World War II.

Well-stocked aid stations are needed to keep riders fueled for high alpine riding. But La Resistance is a ride, not a race; take time to enjoy the scenery.

With views like this, few will mind stopping to repair a puncture,
though the end-of-day party is enticing enough to keep riders rolling.

Riders can choose between 55- and 80-mile routes. Both show off the area's beauty and pass by the National Monument to La Resistance on the Plateau des Glières.

Miles of pedaling are rewarded with hours of dining, drinking, and dancing at La Guinguette.

Ross Muir

La Resistance (LR) promoter

BIKE: "The La Resistance course is an interesting mix of tarmac and coarse alpine gravel and poses an interesting question over equipment choice. A full-on gravel bike with 45mm treaded tires would handle the gravel perfectly but be pretty sluggish on road, particularly the two tough climbs that punctuate the route. On the other hand, a full-on road bike would sail up the climbs (relatively!) but would be difficult to handle on the gravel. I think the ideal compromise is something like the Open U.P. or 3T Exploro with a 28–35mm tire with some tread, giving you speed on tarmac and comfort and handling on the gravel. For the good bike handler or lighter rider, you can go with a narrower tire, and wider for the heavier rider with less finesse! A tubeless wheelset definitely helps, allowing you to run lower pressures whilst avoiding pinch flats."

TIRES: "The famous Clément brand is making a comeback, and they have some great tires for the conditions we encounter around here. My particular favorite is the X'PLOR MSO, which comes in 32, 36 and 40mm and is tubeless ready."

GEARING: "We're a big fan of 1×. Although the gears are a bit gappy, you don't notice it as much off road as you do if you were road racing. And it really simplifies the setup. Gearing obviously depends a lot on fitness. You don't need the super-low gears that you would if you were doing long off-road climbs, as most of the climbing is on tarmac. I've completed the route on my 1× gravel bike with a 36 chainring and an 11–36 cassette, and on my road bike with 50/34 and 11–27."

NUTRITION: "The vibe of LR is one of self-sufficiency, taking your time, and enjoying the ride. We don't have big feed stations every 20 kilometers like some other sportives and gran fondos, where you can grab something on the go. We encourage people to take time to stop, enjoy a coffee and a sandwich, and enjoy the view. We work with the local mountain refuges, which provide a special menu for the riders. To keep you fueled in between those, riders should carry a supply of their own food, be that cheese and ham sandwiches or energy gels."

Gravel Fondo

Black Forest, Germany | October

The creators of Gravel Fondo started with the idea of a two-day social event that would tackle beautiful gravel roads in the legendary mountains of the Black Forest in southwest Germany. Tracks around Feldberg mountain have proven to be perfect for their purposes. Be ready for lots of climbing, though it is evenly spaced throughout the ride, not front- or backloaded. Saturday takes in 48 miles and 6,400 feet of climbing. Sunday is only 37 miles but still packs in a hefty 5,250 feet of climbing.

While Gravel Fondo is a laid-back two-day tour, there are several segments that are timed via Strava, and the fastest riders through those sections win prizes. But the intent of the event is to be fun, "more a social happening than a serious race," as Stephan Geiss, the organizer, puts it.

DEFINING FEATURES

- Two-day social event with packed gravel and a laid-back atmosphere

TRAVEL TIPS

- Zurich and Basel are the closest airports. Stuttgart is also nearby. Baden-Baden is an option, though it's a smaller airport with fewer flights.
- The Black Forest has nicer weather than much of Germany in October, though it can rapidly change when climbing in the hills.
- The University of Freiburg is nearby, and the area is known for its *kuckucksuhren* (cuckoo clocks).
- Accommodation options abound, with camping, dorms, RV parking, and nearby hotels.

Heidelburg
START/FINISH

Black Forest

2,000 FT.

300

MILES 0   10   20   30   40   48

Gravel Fondo in the Black Forest of Germany offers two distances, both with significant climbing.

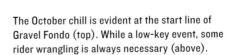

The October chill is evident at the start line of Gravel Fondo (top). While a low-key event, some rider wrangling is always necessary (above).

Gravel Fondo employs Strava to record times over prescribed sections of the route (above). The going can get technical in the Black Forest (right).

Switchback roads, lakeside hangouts, and local cuisine draw in competitors from near and far. If you travel to Freiburg for Gravel Fondo, be sure to set aside time in the city. The area is also famed for its *kuckucksuhren* (cuckoo clocks).

A post-race fire is great for recounting the day's endless exploits.

Stephan Geiss

*Brand manager for Votec Bikes
and creator of Gravel Fondo*

BIKE: "I wanted to make the event accessible to as many people as possible. Gravel biking is just kicking off here in Germany. So the tracks should be doable with a road bike with 25–28mm tires. But Gravel Fondo is definitely most fun with an agile gravel bike, 700c with 35–40mm tires."

TIRES: "Personally, I'm riding the Challenge Gravel Grinder, a tire that is perfectly suited to the conditions in the Black Forest. My background is cyclocross, and I fancy the tan walls. Schwalbe's G-One in either 35 or 40mm size is a great tire for the dense gravel tracks and flowy singletracks."

GEARING: "1×11 with a 40- or 42-tooth chainring in front and a SRAM 10–42 cassette is what we spec on our bike, and it's perfect for the event."

NUTRITION: "The event is not too serious. The layout is more like a ride with friends spiced up with curated Strava segments for those hungry for a challenge. I wanted to serve good food on the track and didn't want the riders to eat packaged space food. We served local ham (Schwarzwälder Schinken) and cheese and nonalcoholic beer."

Gravel Fondo takes advantage of the well-made *wanderwegs*.

Gravel Roc

Fréjus, France | October

If you like the finer things in life, consider a gravel race along France's famous Côte d'Azur, the beautiful Mediterranean coastline in the southeast of the country. Gravel Roc is a new event organized by the Amaury Sport Organisation (ASO), owners of the Tour de France, Dakar Rally, and other iconic sporting events. It takes place alongside the long-running Roc d'Azur mountain bike races and cycling festival.

Although the race is only 50 kilometers (31 miles), it climbs over 2,000 feet, traversing gravel, sand, and a few rocky, technical sections of terrain. In the process, you're treated to views of the Mediterranean Sea and the beautiful coastline that attracts some of the wealthiest vacationers in the world.

DEFINING FEATURES

- 50 kilometers with a mix of road, forest tracks, and technical sections
- Gravel or cyclocross bikes with drop bars are required; mountain bikes are forbidden

TRAVEL TIPS

- The closest international airport is Nice Côte d'Azur, 58 kilometers (36 miles) from Fréjus.
- Rental apartments and campsites are available near the race venue.

If some time on the Riviera sounds good, why not take along your bike and race Gravel Roc?

Pre-race jitters are all part of the fun. Once underway, 30 miles of gravel, sand and rocky riding along the Mediterranean Sea focus a rider's attention.

Frédéric Salomone

*Race director
of the Roc d'Azur*

BIKE: "Both cyclocross and gravel bikes are allowed, but gravel bikes are more adapted for this course."

TIRES: "For Gravel Roc, you need to run tubeless to succeed. A semi-slick tread pattern is a good option."

GEARING: "There are two schools of thought, but 1×11 seems to be the better choice on this course. There are some steep climbs like the Col du Bougnon and some technical sections that are quite bumpy, so you need a low gear."

NUTRITION: "It is not very different from any other type of course. We have five feed stations on the route with food and water."

Exploring areas more than a day's ride away is only a matter of some planning and a set of bikepacking bags.

⑤ MULTIDAY ADVENTURES

With almost limitless miles of dirt roads traversing the world, single-day events can leave some cyclists wanting more. Even when exploring the limits of human-powered travel, you can only cover so much ground in a day. Extending the ride means pushing yourself further. Carrying your necessities on your bike, navigating your way forward, finding something new around every corner—a multiday adventure is a wonderful way to escape your quotidian life in a picturesque setting.

For first timers looking to ride beyond their normal roads, a quick overnighter may be the way to go. To keep things simple, consider a hotel or cabin destination that is

a day's ride away. This will make your load light and the riding fun. Carry a toothbrush and a change of clothes in addition to the normal spares you have on your bicycle.

If you like to camp, try an initial sortie where you carry just enough gear to spend a night under the stars, and buy ready-to-eat food in towns. Start your day with some water and an energy bar, then make your way to a well-deserved breakfast at a café. Little planning tricks like this keep the riding fun and the preparation easy. This approach also eliminates the need to purchase camping gear until you find it absolutely necessary.

However you choose to attempt your first overnight or multiday adventure, keep the priority on fun. Don't overdo it. Your favorite climb can quickly become a real slog with a full load on your bicycle. Be sure to carry a camera or smartphone to take pictures. Taking breaks to catch your breath and admiring the scenery are part of bike touring. And make no bones about it, that's exactly what you're doing. So enjoy it.

Bikepacking

Unlike traditional bicycle touring setups that employ a set of racks and bags that attach to them, usually a pair on the fork and another set flanking the rear wheel, bikepacking was born out of a desire to go light and fast.

Soft luggage bikepacking bags are easy to attach, eliminate trouble-prone racks, and centralize the load. They also keep your bike narrow to maintain maneuverability.

Bikepacking bags are soft luggage that strap directly to a bicycle's frame, saddle/seatpost, and handlebar. This arrangement saves weight and eliminates the possibility of rack failures. It also helps to centralize the load you're carrying, which will maintain your bike's maneuverability better than carrying your gear in outboard panniers or saddlebags. You'll find the difference especially useful on dirt and gravel roads, and when riding on mountain bike trails.

Another upside is that you don't need a touring bike with bosses (called "braze-ons") embedded in the frame that accept rack fittings. Instead, you can use the mountain,

cyclocross, gravel, hybrid, or road bike you already have for your exploring. As mentioned elsewhere in this book, just be sure that your bike is in good working order before you head out. For more information on specific gear, see Chapter 7.

Multiday routes

Although it's easy to create your own routes, especially ones from your front door, there are several established paths already available to gravel adventurers. Some are thoroughly researched and constantly updated. Others are somewhat vague suggestions. In either case, be sure to do your homework so that you don't find yourself without food or—especially—water in remote areas. The Adventure Cycling Association has two dirt road routes, the Great Divide Mountain Bike Route and the Idaho Hot Springs Mountain Bike Route. Other great choices can be found on Bikepacking.com and also on the Bikepacking.net forum.

There are far more routes than there is space here to describe them, but several standouts are outlined in the following pages. Some may appear daunting at first glance, but don't be put off by routes that seem beyond your abilities. Instead, consider touring a section of a given route. This will give you a taste of what's out there and help you prepare for tackling it in its entirety at a later time.

None of the routes here are recommended for first-time bikepackers. Before heading out for a week or more on rugged terrain, you'll want to prepare with over-nighters and long weekend trips. Shorter trips will help you to refine your packing list and how you load your bike, distributing the weight to maintain optimal handling. For instance, some people sleep cold, while others are hot even in cold temperatures. You'll want to know that you have a sleep system that works well before you take off for a month's adventure. Over-nighters let you tweak your system while only risking a single night's discomfort.

It's vitally important to figure out what works for your personal needs and taste through trial and error. Merely copying someone else's packing list is a surefire way to bring misery upon yourself. Instead, use the shared packing lists that you find during your research as a collection of potential gear candidates. See the equipment chapter for a proposed multiday adventure packing list.

You don't need a lot of gear to enjoy the great outdoors. Keep it light and simple, and experiment on short trips first to see what works best for you.

Great Divide Mountain Bike Route

Banff, Alberta, Canada, to Antelope Wells, New Mexico | 2,768 miles

The biggest gravel route of them all is the Great Divide Mountain Bike Route (GDMBR), crisscrossing almost 3,000 miles of America's Continental Divide. The Adventure Cycling Association, with Michael "Mac" McCoy as the head of the project, developed the route over the course of four years of travel and research. It was completed as a border-to-border route in 1998. Created as the longest off-pavement cycling route in the world, it was originally intended for touring cyclists. As with many routes of this length, the course is continually updated as roads and access change. One of those changes was an extension into Canada. Currently the route is 2,768 miles long with 200,000 feet of climbing.

The GDMBR begins in Banff, Alberta, and makes its way through the Rocky Mountains to its southern terminus in Antelope Wells, New Mexico, at the Mexico border. Along the way, it takes in parts of Alberta, British Columbia, Montana, Idaho, Wyoming, Colorado, and New Mexico using pavement, gravel, dirt roads, and short sections of singletrack.

As you might expect, after a route like the GDMBR is assembled, it doesn't take long for someone to race it to establish a record. In 1999, less than a year after the first iteration of the route was completed by McCoy and his Adventure Cycling Association colleagues, legendary ultra-endurance athlete John Stamstad did just that. He raced from the border crossing in Roosville, Montana, the northern terminus at the time, south to Antelope Wells in 18 days and 5 hours.

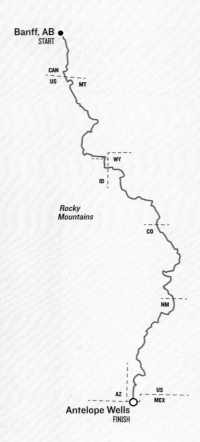

Chris Plesko powers his single-speed mountain bike along a remote section of the GDMBR.

Challenges along the Great Divide take on many forms. But the diverse beauty rewards the struggle. Jay Petervary takes a deserved break (opposite left). Craig Stappler and Ollie Whalley pedal through Aspen Alley near the Wyoming/Colorado border (left). The cockpit on Mike Hall's bike is organized chaos (right).

Wide open spaces abound.
Flooded road sections are
routine, especially in the
Canadian section (above).
Good lights and warm
clothes are needed to ensure
comfortable night riding (left).

John Stamstad

THE GREAT DIVIDE'S RECORD-SETTING PIONEER

There are few ultramarathon cycling legends like John Stamstad. Though a soft-spoken man, his claims to fame are illustrious. He is a member of the Mountain Bike Hall of Fame, inducted in 2000. During his 15 years as a professional mountain bike racer, Stamstad established several benchmarks. In 1992, with funding from Bridgestone Bicycles, he traveled to Australia to race across the 3,500-mile width of the country, including the formidable Outback. This marked the first crossing of the Australian continent by bicycle.

Stamstad dominated the Iditasport, a bicycle race along the famous Iditarod Trail in Alaska, from 1993 through 1996. He then carried on, winning the even tougher Iditasport Extreme from 1997 through 2000. In 1996, Stamstad was the first mountain biker to take on the 24 Hours of Canaan as a solo competitor. To do so, he entered the relay using four variations of his name. In 1997, a solo category was created.

Stamstad continued to search for ultracycling challenges, and with the creation of the Great Divide Mountain Bike Route, he hit upon the idea of racing its length to establish a time.

"I love that people still do the Divide, and that other people have gotten to enjoy the route."

How much research did you do beforehand?

There wasn't a whole lot of research to be able to do. The maps were brand new. They were full of errors. I spent a ton of time stopped, attempting to navigate. Which is fine. Somebody has to do that. The reason the maps are so good now is because a bunch of people rode the route and figured out where there were some issues.

I was intending on doing the route fully supported. I was going to have full vehicle support and do it as a fastest time possible. But then, the more I thought about it, the person who does something like this first really sets a precedent. I thought that wasn't the way this route should be done. I thought it should be done a little bit more organically.

I decided to do it on my own just a week before I left. That did not give me any time to prepare. I didn't mail out anything [supplies sent ahead along the route for pick up]. I had a week to research doing it totally unsupported. That's a whole different can of worms. So I had to scramble. You can't prepare logistically for a 2,500-mile route in a week, at least not optimally. But I still feel that it was absolutely the right thing to do.

I found food. I didn't find great food. I relied on gas station food a lot more than I would have liked. If I had prepared for it, I would have sent some good, healthy energy drinks and protein drinks to post offices or bike shops along the way. Or you send them to a hotel so that you can get them 24/7.

In deciding how to go about establishing the record, I spent years talking with a number of people about how we should do these things. What constitutes a record? Let's agree on a set of rules. After a lot of discussion with many of the top guys, I thought the best set of rules is to have no rules. If you can't enforce the rules, then don't have them. There's always going

John Stamstad tried a trailer in an attempt to distribute weight more evenly on the Iditasport Extreme's soft snow.

Stamstad stops at a mandatory overnight during the Iditasport Extreme.

to be a trust factor. There are no security cameras out there. So if somebody wanted to hop in a car and get a ride, they certainly could. You just have to trust that the people who do these sorts of things are [not] those types of folks, and there isn't enough financial incentive to make it worthwhile for somebody to cheat themselves. I think it's a very honorable sport.

Who were some of those other guys you spoke with?
Mike Curiak, for sure. He was one of the top guys at the time. Pat Norwil, who I used to race against a lot. I tried to involve the folks who were relevant at the time.

Did you pre-ride any sections?
No. Nothing. I'd never seen any of the route.

Tell us about your bike.
I used an Airborne titanium hardtail with a suspension fork. Shimano XTR components. Totally conventional for bikes of the day. It was the same bike that I used for 24-hour racing. I certainly wouldn't use that bike if I were to do it again. These days I'm sure everyone rides a fully rigid 29er.

I have the new modern bikepacking bags now, and they are a thousand times better than anything that was available back then. I used a rack, but I didn't trust any pannier not to break. So I took a waterproof dry bag and strapped it to a rear rack. I had a front handlebar bag and a small frame bag for grabbing snacks. But most of my gear was on top of a rack in a dry bag.

What gear did you carry? Tent? Bivy? Other essentials?
I could more than cut my weight in half using modern materials. I had state-of-the-art equipment, but I had a 2-pound sleeping

bag and a 2-pound bivy sack. I had a Gore-Tex jacket that even after cutting the hood off was still 16 ounces. Now you wouldn't carry a jacket that weighs more than 8 ounces.

That's where gear is fun. That's what has made bikepacking approachable. If you have to do panniers, riding off-road, carrying a few-pound tent and heavy sleeping bag, it's not a fun sport. Whereas when you cut that weight in half, now all of a sudden almost anyone can do it. Not everyone is going to do the Divide, but everyone can do an overnight. You can put it on a bike and go.

With the new bags, you can ride technical trails. With old-school panniers, you can't. You're not putting low-riders on a mountain bike and riding singletrack very well.

What other essentials?

I didn't carry a spare tire. I carried a good boot in case I shredded a tire. A bunch of tubes. The usual kit that you would pack on any length ride in terms of tools. I didn't carry anything special. I didn't carry a stove. I carried a CamelBak for water. I could carry 200 ounces plus of water. That was fine.

The one thing I didn't bring that I should have was a shock pump. I blew my fork in Montana on day three. It's not that big a deal to ride with a flat fork, but the problem is that it changes your saddle position, and your bike's handling changes a lot. It drops the front end a couple inches and throws off the geometry a couple of degrees. That messes up your riding position, and that messes up your biomechanics. I couldn't get a new cartridge for my fork until Steamboat Springs, Colorado, so I had to ride 600 miles on a flat fork. I wasn't thrilled about that. That was extremely uncomfortable. It was a brand of fork that I had raced on a ton. I never once had a single issue. Never

Stamstad won every solo 24 Hours of Canaan from 1996 through 2000.

blew one. And then something that's never happened before tends to happen.

I had a NiteRider with a 5-watt halogen bulb powered by five D-cell batteries. And you have to carry two sets of those because they don't last an entire night. So that's 10 D-cell batteries. That's probably 5 pounds right there. Whereas now, light technology has gone crazy in the last five years. They weigh nothing. You can have as many lumens as you want.

Did you encounter any problems along the way? Punctures, mechanicals, rabid dogs?

Tons of flats. I ran tubes at the time. I remember one stretch going into Rawlins, Wyoming. Mosquitos were a huge problem. I don't mean one or two mosquitos pestering you. I mean all exposed skin is covered in mosquitos. I had this one flat, and I had to change the flat while running because mosquitos can only fly so fast. So I stopped to change the tire, and I was covered in mosquitos. I was worried that I wouldn't make it through the next day if my body was covered in mosquito bites. One or two is no problem, but a hundred bites could be an issue.

So I had to change a flat while running down a dirt road. I ran back and forth trying to change it while I was running. Then I quickly put the wheel back on my bike and got rolling. That was irritating.

How did you certify your time?
It was the honor system. I made sure to note when I left the Canadian border and when I arrived at the Mexican border. Of course, I would make phone calls to loved ones. There was a traceable record. I would try to call once a day, whenever I hit a town. That was the best technology at the time.

What did your record mean to you at the time? What are your thoughts on Mike Hall's 2016 record?
I think point-to-point records are valid, especially [on] any new trail, anywhere on the planet. That is legitimate to set a standard for others to beat. What I really liked about the Divide was that, at the time, I did not know of anyone who had done an off-road bike event, of any type, that long and arduous. So it was new territory. I didn't know how long the Divide would take me. So you can't even ballpark a time frame. How many days can I go with a couple hours' sleep a night? That intrigued me, motivated me. What can the body do? I was the guinea pig.

It's nice seeing the sport evolve. People get faster, and that's satisfying too. I love that people still do the Divide, and that other people have gotten to enjoy the route. That's probably the best thing. Lots have raced it, but a ton more have ridden the Divide just for the heck of it. I think that's phenomenal.

Were you happy with your ride as a first attempt on the route?
I was really happy with my effort. I was super fit when I did it. I was very frustrated with navigation. I spent a lot of time not knowing which way to turn at the crossroad of two dirt roads where nothing is marked. That also determines how little sleep you can get by with, because when you're doing full-on navigation, you need to have a sound mind. And that means you need to sleep a little more. Whereas, if you don't have to think, you can go on a lot less sleep.

I had a couple mornings where I would wake up after finishing the previous day in the dark. I'd wake up a couple hours later, and you think you know where you're going but it turns out you're going in the opposite direction. Your mind is a little soft. I had a few of those mornings where you ride up a 3-mile pass and it's not the one you want to be riding up. That's mentally defeating. That really tosses you.

Have you returned and ridden the Great Divide since your record ride?
I used to be an outside sales rep, and I used to drive through certain parts of Montana and Wyoming near the route. I haven't ridden on the route, though.

What advice do you have for others looking to test their limits through ultracycling?
The key is just to have fun. I did it because it was fun for me. I think the sense of adventure is the most important part. Go out and explore something. With some decent equipment and a little bit of fitness, there is a ton that you can explore that the average person will never see. I think that the beauty of it is the access.

The Tour Divide

In 2004, another ultra-endurance athlete, Mike Curiak, created the Great Divide Race. Along with six other competitors, Curiak raced from the Canadian border south to Antelope Wells. In the process, he established a new record of 16 days, 57 minutes, taking more than two days off Stamstad's effort.

From there, the race continued to evolve along with the route. In 2005, the Great Divide Race started in Banff, reflecting the Adventure Cycling Association's updates. It was now organized by Pete Basinger, a participant in the previous year's event. In 2008, the race was taken over by Matthew Lee and renamed the Tour Divide. Conceived as a solo self-supported effort, the rules are straightforward. No outside support is allowed. That means no drafting, no support crew. Racers can ship supplies to themselves, but only using the U.S. Postal Service's general delivery system. All commercial services that are equally available along the route are allowed. There is no entry fee and no prize money.

Racers carry GPS-enabled tracking devices to ensure they stay on the prescribed course. Friends and family can follow along on the Trackleaders.com website. The majority of racers meet in Banff and head south starting the second week of June to make use of the long days.

Racers can also start at any time to attempt an individual time trial (ITT) of the course. In either case, both northbound and southbound, the clock runs the entire time, only stopping when the rider crosses the finish line. The current record is held by Mike Hall of the United Kingdom, who in 2016 covered 2,713 miles in an amazing 13 days, 22 hours, and 51 minutes, averaging 194.1 miles per day. In a tragic loss to his family, loved ones, and the ultracycling community, Hall was struck by a car and killed while vying for victory in the inaugural 2017 Indian Pacific Wheel Race, a 3,400-mile unsupported race across Australia. The race was canceled, and a memorial ride in Sydney drew hundreds of cyclists.

Mike Curiak makes his way through the southwestern terrain.

Interestingly, there is an interplay between the Adventure Cycling Association and the racers who tackle the Great Divide Route. Matthew Lee, organizer of the Tour Divide and multiple-time champion of the route, proposed and then pieced together a rugged section that extended the course into Canada. The Flathead and Wigwam river valleys are among the wildest in Canada, and including them brings racers into a remote area while adding almost 40 miles to the route. The extension was first raced in 2009 and now acts as part of the official GDMBR.

Lael Wilcox

PERPETUAL TRAVELER

Lael Wilcox made a splash in the ultra-endurance world when in 2015, she raced the Great Divide not once, but twice. Each time she set records and placed herself among the top 10 fastest finishers in the history of the Tour Divide. Typically racing in a favorite T-shirt, Wilcox went on to race and win the overall at the 2016 Trans Am Bike Race, a self-supported road race across the United States. Previously she has toured in Africa, Israel, and eastern Europe. She and her partner, Nicholas Carman, live their life almost perpetually on the road, touring all over the world with breaks for races and time with family. When contacted for this interview, Wilcox and Carman were in Bishop, California, resting after a blistering crossing of Death Valley.

"Touring is fun because you have more time. You can take your time and enjoy the place where you are."

Where do you call home? How much time do you spend on the road each year?

Anchorage, Alaska, is home. Only a couple months. This year I was in Alaska for two months and I worked at a shop for one month. Mostly I'm moving around, but I get back at least once every year to visit my family.

The rest of the time I'm riding, both touring and racing. I used to spend more like six months in a place, working. But since I started endurance racing I've focused on that and been working less. And I love it. It's great. Really, the touring is what I love the most. I like the racing too, but it's pretty exhausting. Seeing new places, sleeping in different places every night, and riding is what I like.

Do you prefer dirt and gravel riding to pavement?

Definitely. I do like road riding, but as far as touring and traveling in different countries, I'd rather be on dirt. The camping is better. The riding is usually more fun. You end up in more remote areas and definitely see a different part of the world.

What draws you to routes like the Great Divide?

The Great Divide is epic, especially racing it as Tour Divide. It's just mountain pass after pass. I love climbing. That style of riding is great for me. Otherwise, once routes exist, I just want to see where they go. You see that it starts and ends at different points, but I want to see what happens in between. So that's led me to the Great Divide, the Arizona Trail, a dirt route in South Africa called the Dragon's Spine. Israel has a great route called the Holyland Challenge. They're working on a cross-country mountain bike route as well. So knowing that a route exists will draw me to a new place.

What tips do you have for people new to gravel or those considering riding the Great Divide?

You really don't need that much equipment. Keeping your bike and your equipment light will make your riding a lot more fun. Starting off, people tend to bring a lot more than they need. So minimizing your gear and your layers, even opting to have a lighter sleeping bag and lighter equipment, can really help a lot. Get out there and see if it's for you.

You don't have to race to be out there. People are often drawn to the Tour Divide or these long-distance races when they've never even gone on a regular bike trip. I recommend going out for a bike trip first and enjoying it. Sleeping as much as you want. Taking the days as they come. Being able to take a day off if the weather is bad. Get out there and do that first. And then, if you want to translate that into racing, you'll do so much better.

Any tips specifically for female riders?

Know that there's nothing to be afraid of. There's no danger in being alone. Especially on a route like the Divide. It's very safe. Just go out and do it. People may tell you not to or advise against it, but go out and prove them wrong.

As far as the racing goes, women have just looked at racing within the women's category. And I don't think that that's necessary. I think for endurance racing, the women can compete with the men. I feel like they should go after those times in that race and try to be the overall winner instead of just the women's winner. Because I truly believe that people come to these races with different skills and different abilities. I don't think that it matters if you're a man or a woman. You can compete. Just go for it.

Snug in a sleeping bag, dreaming of a race win.

How do you train for a race like Tour Divide or Trans Am Bike Race?

It's funny, because I really don't do any specific training. Often I don't even ride fast before a race. I don't really feel that I need to. I just ride all the time and usually feel fit for the race.

The past few races, the thing that I've done is to ride to the start. I get a lot of miles in right before the race. That way, I'm really comfortable with my bike. Then I take a couple weeks off, and then I'm ready to go. The first Tour Divide, I rode from Anchorage to the start in Banff. That was actually a pretty long ride, about 2,100 miles. Then I took 10 days off, and then I raced.

Do you have favorite gear or any packing tips you'd like to share?

Yeah! I use a Western Mountaineering summer-weight sleeping bag. I really love those. They're super light, but you also get the most warmth for the weight. That's a favorite.

All the bags on my bike are Revelate Designs, which have been awesome for me. For racing, I usually bring a bivy bag instead of a tent.

When we're touring, we carry a Big Agnes Seedhouse tent, an awesome tent for two people. Totally weatherproof.

For a bivy, I've used a Western Mountaineering vapor barrier. It's technically a sleeping bag liner, but it is weatherproof.

This past race, I got a pair of Patagonia Alpine Houdini pants for use as rain pants. Those are awesome, pack really small, and are easy to move in. Those are my coldest weather layer. Usually I bring a pair of long johns and a pair of rain pants. Often I'll also carry a down vest because it packs really small but adds a lot of warmth.

What does holding the women's Tour Divide record of 15 days, 10 hours (and 7th fastest-ever time) mean to you?

The first time, when I raced Tour Divide in late June, I was really sick. All the way through Montana, for over a week, I was having really bad breathing problems. I had to ride shorter days than I wanted to. So I really didn't perform the way I wanted to. I was pretty happy that I finished, though. After that ride, I had taken two days off the women's record, but I knew that I could ride faster.

My second attempt, I actually wanted to break the men's record, and I was on pace to do that five days in. But then I got stuck in the mud outside Lima, Montana. So I lost that

opportunity. I still finished and rode well and took another two days off my record. I was pretty happy with that, but I feel like there's still room to go faster.

It's a game. The second time I rode the Great Divide was an ITT [individual time trial]. So I was out there by myself just trying to break the record. That's mentally tough. It's really hard to be alone, to have nobody else doing what you're doing. If the weather turns or something goes wrong, you feel like you're just racing time. So it doesn't really matter, nobody really cares, if you have a hard time in the process. In the head-to-head race context, it's a lot more fun because everybody is out there dealing with the same elements and competing.

Now, if anything, I'm more into the race aspect, racing other people instead of racing for the fastest time.

Do you prefer to race or to tour? What are the upsides and downsides to each?

Touring is fun because you have more time. You can take your time and enjoy the place where you are.

The aspect of racing that I really enjoy is that you're passing through so much country so fast and seeing so much every day. You spend so much time awake and outside. I like that as well. It's just less sustainable.

Do you and Nick plan to continue your on-the-road lifestyle for the foreseeable future?

Yes, we've always said that we'll keep doing it as long as it's fun and as long as we want to keep going. We've been traveling like this for nine years now. And it seems to only be getting better. The method of travel or who we're including or sharing experiences with is always developing. It's been a lot of fun.

It's still a big world from the seat of a bicycle. Oregon has miles—days, even—of dirt and gravel roads.

OTHER NOTABLE MULTIDAY ROUTES

While the Great Divide is alluring to most bikepackers and many gravel riders, it is by no means the only long-distance gravel adventure to try. New routes are developed each year, and in some cases old routes are rediscovered. History plays a part in all roads. Knowing the reason why they were constructed, when, and by whom can add to the attraction of a particular journey. The following pages describe several long routes of varying distances, all with fantastic history.

Denali Highway

Paxson, Alaska, to Cantwell, Alaska | Up to 135 miles

If you're looking for remote roads, few places deliver quite like Alaska. The Denali Highway (Alaska Route 8), from Paxson to Cantwell, offers over 100 miles of graded dirt and undulating terrain. Before the construction of the Parks Highway, Denali Highway served as the only access to Denali National Park. Thanks to the newer road, Denali Highway is now rarely traveled, making it ideal for cyclists. Much of the land flanking the road is public, and campsites abound. The Alaska Range, with its peaks and glaciers, forms the background for this ride. Much of the highway is above tree line, so the views are breathtakingly expansive. The highway's highest point is MacLaren Summit at 4,086 feet, the second-highest highway pass in Alaska.

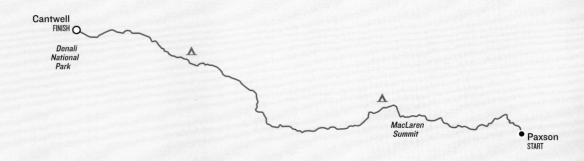

The Alaska Range, with peaks ranging from 11,670 to 20,310 feet, is a stunning backdrop to the Denali Highway.

A quiet dirt road with expansive views is guaranteed to bring a smile to the face of every cyclist.

Few places match the remoteness of Alaska. If considering the Denali Highway, do your homework. Cyclists and hikers must be bear aware and take precautions.

Trans North California

Reno, Nevada, to Mendocino, California | Up to 400 miles

From Reno to Mendocino, the Trans North California route crosses both the Sierras and the Coast Range over its 400 miles and 40,000 feet of climbing. It traverses both the Tahoe and Mendocino National Forests and avoids large cities completely. Each October, an informal race is run using Tour Divide rules and Spot tracking. Expect vast temperature variations any time of year thanks to big elevation and climate zone transitions. If touring the route is more appealing than racing, it can be ridden as long as snow hasn't lingered in the Sierras and you don't mind intense heat in the Central Valley. Organizers of the race encourage participants to be aware of bears, mountain lions, and rattlesnakes. Carrying a way to purify water is also mandatory. As with the Great Divide, a rigid mountain bike with low gearing and tough tires is recommended.

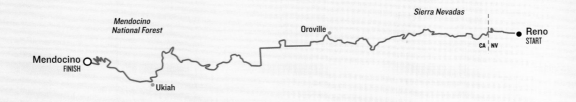

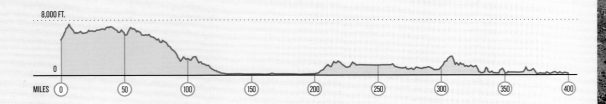

Crossing the state of California means a wide range of terrain and plenty of top-notch views, including this overlook above Verdi, Nevada.

Forest roads in the Sierra Nevada Mountains don't disappoint, but they do challenge even the strongest legs (above). High elevations retain snow longer in the year too. So time your ride well and consider carrying a pair of waterproof socks (right). While the route can be raced, touring it may be more fun. Take time to verify navigation during breaks (opposite).

The Trans California route traverses all manner
of road: paved, dirt, gravel, and singletrack.
Be fit and ready for the occasional hike-a-bike
or portage before taking it on (above). The
Mendocino coast rewards all the tribulations of
getting there (above right). Bear Creek is one
of many places where filtering water is possible.
(below right).

Covering big miles means long days in the saddle. Sunsets and sunrises like this one over Stampede Reservoir near Truckee often bookend memorable bikepacking trips (left). Take your time during precarious sections (above).

Oregon Outback

Klamath Falls, Oregon, to the Deschutes River, Oregon | Up to 364 miles

Although only run as an organized race for one year, the route of the Oregon Outback is still a bikepacker's dream. Over 350 miles of rugged Oregon roads, gravel, and deteriorated double track test even seasoned cyclists. More than 14,000 feet of climbing await, and 75 percent of the route is gravel. The route builders recommend six days to complete the south to north endeavor. Bisecting the state, the Outback begins in Klamath Falls and heads through the Fremont-Winema National Forest, crossing the windy Columbia River Gorge before making its way to its terminus near The Dalles. It's recommended that the Outback be ridden during spring and early summer months, after snow has melted and before the scorching heat of central Oregon hits. Fall is another good time to hit the route. Two-inch-wide tires and low gearing are recommended, though it has been successfully completed on narrower tires.

6,000 FT.

0

MILES 0   50   100   150   200   250   300   350 364

The long, steep climb out of the ghost town of **Ashwood** swallows riders in the forest.

Lush meadows along Five Mile Creek make camping a treat (left). Riders share the first 50 miles with herds of cattle and thousands of birds that flock to the meandering Sprague River (top). Stream crossings are rideable if you're brave enough (right).

Crossing a state aboard a bicycle is a unique way to appreciate the way geography transitions from one area to another. Deserts routinely give way to alpine regions in Oregon. At right: The undulating hills of Rajneeshpuram and Horse Heaven.

Katy Trail

Clinton, Missouri, to Machens, Missouri | Up to 237 miles

As the longest rail-trail in the United States, the Katy Trail is a 237-mile gravel path from Clinton to Machens, Missouri. With the exception of road crossings, there is no car traffic to contend with, making the Katy Trail a great choice for new bicycle travelers. More than half the trail follows Lewis and Clark's pioneering route across the western United States. The trail is also included in the Adventure Cycling Association's Lewis and Clark Route. With gentle undulating terrain, the Katy Trail is great to tackle in sections or ride in its entirety. Bed-and-breakfasts, breweries, restaurants, and wineries have all begun catering to traveling cyclists along much of the trail's length. A good portion of the route rolls along the banks of the Missouri River, offering shade from hot midwestern summer temperatures. While certainly challenging, the surface of the Katy Trail is maintained well enough that road bikes with wide tires, touring bikes, cyclocross, and gravel bikes are all appropriate. In short, the Katy Trail is a great choice for all cyclists and their ambitions.

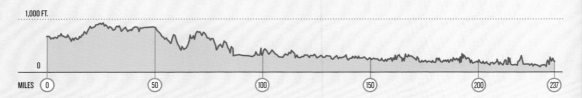

The Katy Trail is a lovely rail-trail with 237 miles of smooth gravel and gentle grades.

Cyclists on the Katy Trail get the pleasure of passing through several tunnels along the former railroad bed.

Reflectors are an essential safety addition for night-mowing chores (left). Here and there, the Missouri River has carved stone cliffs that tower above the trail (below left).

Most of the Katy Trail follows the winding curves of the Missouri River. Bridges are a common sight and crossing them a common occurrence.

Elevations are not high on the Katy Trail and relief is also minimal. With little reason to stand, you'll want a comfortable saddle (above right). Businesses on the Katy Trail increasingly cater to touring cyclists (below).

Great Allegheny Passage and C&O Towpath

Pittsburgh, Pennsylvania, to Washington, D.C. | Up to 335 miles

The midwestern and western United States are not the only places that offer days of gravel riding. Extensive dirt and gravel routes dot the eastern states too. One of the most notable is the Great Allegheny Passage (GAP), a 150-mile trail built primarily on the abandoned railway beds of the Western Maryland Railway and the Pittsburgh and Lake Erie Railroad. Like Missouri's Katy Trail, this route is not open to motorized traffic, making it attractive to new cyclists or those seeking quiet. The Great Allegheny Passage runs southeast between Pittsburgh and Cumberland, Maryland, and can be connected with the C&O Towpath for a 335-mile journey ending in Washington, D.C. While in Pennsylvania, the route runs near Fallingwater, the iconic home designed by legendary American architect Frank Lloyd Wright. Many camping options as well as bed-and-breakfasts, restaurants, and other services cater to cyclists on the GAP. With its groomed gravel surface, virtually any bike with adequate gearing and reliable tires is up to the trail.

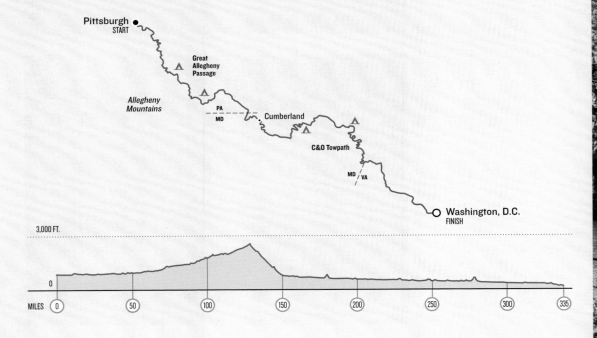

The Riverton Bridge, built in 1891, crosses the Allegheny River in Pennsylvania and is part of the Great Allegheny Passage.

Point State Park in Pittsburgh signals the meeting of the Allegheny and Monongahela Rivers and the beginning of both the Ohio River and the Great Allegheny Passage (above). Cucumber Falls are a serene scene in Ohiopyle State Park, Pennsylvania (left). Big Savage Vista lives up to its name (right).

Much of the GAP is a leafy, green tunnel, bordered in some places by intricate rock outcroppings (above). The ornate Bollman Bridge near Meyersdale, Pennsylvania, was built in 1871 and is now used by the GAP (right).

Built in 1912, the Ohiopyle High Bridge crosses over the Youghiogheny River (left). At the Pennsylvania/Maryland border, cyclists also cross the Mason-Dixon line (top). The Pinkerton Tunnel was reopened in late 2015 for use by cyclists along the GAP (above).

Many parts of the Colorado Trail involve pushing your bike rather than riding. But don't let that deter you!

SINGLETRACK
MULTIDAY ROUTES

While the focus of this book is on gravel and dirt road riding, there are several singletrack routes worthy of mention. These are rugged trails where a mountain bike is recommended. But they are often ridden and raced by the same people who tackle the Great Divide Route. If you are looking for technically challenging riding, look no further. While certainly not the only two trails of this length, the Colorado Trail and the Arizona Trail have gained fame, and perhaps notoriety, in the ultra-endurance world, serving as part of the Triple Crown that includes those two plus the Tour Divide.

Colorado Trail (CT)

Waterton Canyon, Colorado, to Durango, Colorado | Up to 525 miles

Completed in 1987, the 525-mile mountain bike version of this spectacular route winds its way between southwest Denver and Durango. Whether touring or racing, mountain bikers huff and puff their way through 70,000 feet of climbing through the rarified Rocky Mountain air. From trail's inception, mountain bikers have had access to the entirety of the route, with the exception of several wilderness areas that justifiably remain off limits. It was first raced in 2007, and the current course record is held by Neil Beltchenko with a time of 3 days, 19 hours, and 50 minutes. For more information on the trail, including maps, guidebook, and databook, head to ColoradoTrail.org. For more details, go to www.climbingdreams.net/ctr/.

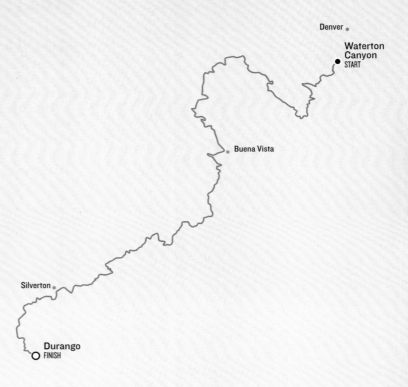

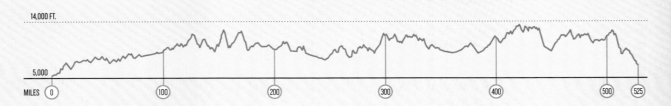

This is the stuff that a mountain biker's dreams are made of: a ribbon of singletrack and all day to ride it.

Aspens give shade to a singletrack section along the Colorado Trail (left). Signage is frequent but note that cyclists must detour around wilderness areas (above). Other segments of the Colorado Trail use two-track mountain roads (right).

The benefits of bikepacking include camp spots that are far from parking lots and crowds of tourists (above). While it's easy to get bogged down in the effort, take time to look up and around while on the CT (right).

Depending on the timing of your trip, wildflowers can be found in abundance on the Colorado Trail (top). Summer sunsets in the Rocky Mountains are hard to beat (above).

Rugged sections of trail are not uncommon on the CT. Bring good walking shoes (above left). The sun makes a great clothes dryer and electronics charger if you plan ahead (above right).

The Columbine, state flower of Colorado, can be seen along the trail in spring. Take photos but don't pick; they're protected by law.

Arizona Trail (AZT)

Sierra Vista, Arizona, to Kaibab Plateau, Arizona | Up to 739 miles

Bisecting the state of Arizona, the two termini of this arduous route are the Mexico border in the south and the state line with Utah in the north. The trail stretches 739 miles in total, including a 24-mile rim-to-rim hike across the Grand Canyon, where mountain bikers are required to dismantle their bikes and carry them. In most cases, racers take off both wheels and pedals, then strap everything to a hydration pack. While officially completed in 2011, the route was accessible as early as 2002. Scott Morris first raced the AZT in its entirety in 2005. The next year, he established a time for a shorter, 300-mile version of the route. The 750-route record is held by Neil Beltchenko at 6 days, 12 hours, and 28 minutes. Kurt Refsnider holds the record for the 300-mile route at 1 day, 21 hours, 7 minutes. For more information on the trail and the race, head to aztrail.org and topofusion.com/azt/.

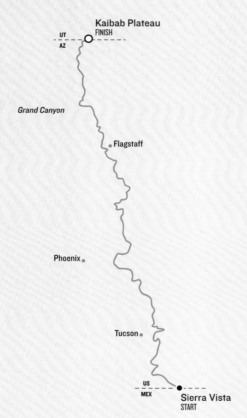

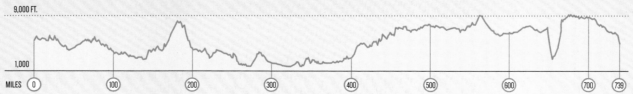

The Arizona Trail is a beautifully rugged route where water is scarce and views are endless.

Completing the entire 739-mile Arizona Trail includes dismantling your bicycle and carrying it the 24 miles across the Grand Canyon. Be sure to practice before leaving home (left). The prickly nature of the Arizona Trail is obvious. Install sturdy tires before heading out (above). Gila monsters, the largest lizards native to the U.S., can be found in many parts of Arizona (right).

Wildflowers break up the reds, browns, and greys of desert (above). A giant saguaro cactus can reach as high as 60 feet and weigh well over a ton in wet years (right).

While trees may be in short supply in some areas, stunning and improbable rock formations populate the Arizona Trail in abundance.

Whether you keep it minimal or prefer a tent, planning will make any trip smoother.

PLANNING YOUR OWN MULTIDAY ROUTE

Some say that adventure begins when something goes wrong. It's perhaps hard to argue with that, but that doesn't mean that you should leave everything to chance when heading out for a multiday trip. Preparations should include taking the time to know your route, the terrain, and weather, as well as services along the way. While a flat tire on a deserted road can lead to a good story, not having a spare tube and the appropriate tools to install and inflate it will make for a miserable time. Likewise, it's normal to get a bit hungry or thirsty while riding, but severe dehydration is a potentially lethal matter that should be taken seriously. Taking time to learn where you can camp or lodge as well as where water and food are sold is precious information.

For more advice on route planning, a professional like Mac McCoy is happy to share. As a seasoned cartographer and the creator of the Great Divide Mountain Bike Route, McCoy's credentials are hard to beat. McCoy's eyes were opened to the possibilities of bicycle travel, especially through national forests, after spending a couple of summers in the early 1980s surveying every road that had been constructed in the Yaak Ranger District of the Kootenai National Forest in northwest Montana. Riding a small motorcycle over the hundreds of miles of forest tracks and decommissioned logging roads planted a seed that bore fruit years later, when McCoy worked for the Adventure Cycling Association. See the sidebar for his thoughts on planning a ride in a new area.

Planning tips from Mac McCoy

As the creator of the Great Divide route, Mac McCoy has a passion for adventure. While these pieces of advice are written with the United States in mind, the principles apply to overseas trips as well.

STEP ONE: Prowl around Crazy Guy on a Bike (crazyguyonabike.com), where you'll find journals from cyclists who have toured in just about every corner of the country and the globe. Other good resources for inspiration and route ideas include the Adventure Cycling Association Forums (forums .adventurecycling.org), BikeOvernights.org, and crowdsourced mapping sites like MapMyRide.com and RideWithGPS.com.

STEP TWO: Contact those in the know. These folks include state bicycle/pedestrian coordinators, national forest offices and other public land agencies, bike shop personnel, and local/regional bike club members. Some of these people will be familiar with the roads you're thinking of riding on and can tell you what is or is not a good idea. Again, Adventure Cycling Association maintains an active list of member clubs: adventurecycling .org/resources/member-clubs.

STEP THREE: Search for traffic flow maps covering the region you plan to cycle in, and use them in conjunction with a state road map and/or atlas, such as the DeLorme state gazetteers. Doing so can help you eliminate roads that carry large amounts of motorized traffic, which is particularly useful in the East and Midwest, where there are a lot of paved roads. They also often indicate road surfaces. As you plot your route, be attentive to the populations of the towns it will take you through. This will provide a good idea of the services available, or lack thereof.

Mac and Nancy McCoy, first bikepacking trip, western Wyoming, 1985.

Lael Wilcox gives her tidy bikepacking setup the onceover in Mexico. Tuck your gear inside your bags whenever possible, not strapped to the outside.

6 OUTFITTING YOUR BIKE

Almost any bicycle can be used for gravel riding, or even gravel racing. Most important is that it's in good working order and fits its rider. Don't let doubts about the bike hanging in your garage deter you from trying that dirt road that's always intrigued you. Give it a go. Bikes are usually far more capable than we realize. In many cases, a road bike with robust tires will be fine, and a mountain bike will always plow through whatever you may encounter.

Mountain bikes, fatbikes, and cyclocross bikes will all work for gravel riding throughout the United States. Road bikes with clearance for 28mm tires are up to the task in many areas. Again, if you have anything resembling a serviceable bike, try it on your local dirt and gravel roads before you lay out a lot of cash on a more expensive rig.

If you'd like to have a specific bike for your dirt road needs, there are loads of options. If you're on a budget, look at used bikes. There's a burgeoning market out there where high-end bikes from 10 years ago can be purchased cheaply. You don't need whiz-bang technology to ride gravel. In fact, in some cases, the newest components don't work as reliably in gravel conditions as older versions.

Also consider that whenever you spend money on something with multiple uses, you can double your return on the expense, or more. Although one bike may not be perfectly suited to every use, gravel riding isn't the Tour de France, where small differences have large consequences. It's a forgiving sport. With the right adventurous spirit, it's likely that a single bike can cover all of your cycling needs, from trail riding to gravel roads to pavement.

On the other hand, the alternative—having a series of bikes with designated ride purposes—does not mean that you've been duped. Owning lots of bikes is a lot of fun. Discovering the capabilities of your bikes, and extending them with different component choices and improved skills, is a lifelong pursuit that brings many cyclists great joy.

Bike fit

Whatever choice you make, whatever your situation, seek help regarding bike fit. Any shop worth visiting will offer assistance in this area. If you have cycling friends with loads of experience or, ideally, a nearby shop or an individual who specializes in bike fit, pay a visit and pay for that time. A personalized bike fit is not the exclusive bastion of professional cyclists. Every rider can benefit from the expertise of a qualified specialist. New riders in particular can avoid months, perhaps years, of discomfort by getting a bike fit when beginning to ride. Experienced riders can address nagging issues and find increased comfort with the expertise of a bike fitter.

Literally starting from the ground up, a professional fitter will often begin by ensuring that your cycling shoes are the correct size and have the correct support. From there, pedal selection and cleat position are addressed based on your personal dimensions and physiological tendencies. Saddle choice is another important area where a fitter can save time, money, and discomfort. The size of your bicycle frame is checked to ensure that you are aboard a bike that suits you. Saddle height and fore/aft position are then determined. Even saddle tilt is given close attention.

Once the power-producing components are dialed in, the focus moves forward. The reach to the handlebars and their height are adjusted via the stem. Handlebar shape and drop, and brake/shift lever position are explored. These items affect how you sit on the bicycle, how upright or inclined forward you are. With a comfortable, efficient position, you will avoid injury and develop a powerful pedal stroke while avoiding strains and aches.

Most cyclists fit off-the-rack bicycles. Unless you are extremely tall or extremely short, a custom bike isn't typically necessary from a biomechanical perspective. An experienced bike fitter can nearly always find a range of frames with the right proportions for you to consider.

Once you have a bike that is the right size, focus on contact points. These include shorts, saddle, shoes, pedals, gloves, handlebars, and handlebar tape. Everything that serves as an interface between rider and machine is important. Assuming your bike is in good working order, you want to spend your money on these items. As an example, a high-end rear derailleur doesn't shift significantly better than a cheaper version, but spending a bit extra to get the right saddle will improve your ride experience enormously.

This is also where bike fit comes back into play. An experienced fitter can often make educated suggestions based on previous experience, the kind of rides you enjoy, your flexibility and build. Often bike shops will have test saddles that you can try before buying. If not, many will accept returns within a certain time frame. These programs can take the financial risk out of saddle shopping.

A fitter can also help you avoid the cost of buying multiple stems or handlebars while you experiment to find a good position or a comfortable shape. The upfront cost of a bike fit, even if the bill tops a couple hundred dollars, is well worth it both financially and in the invaluable realm of injury prevention. Pain-free cycling is much more likely to lead to smiles. It is also safer, as the rider can focus on the road ahead and not the twinge in his or her knee.

During discussions with your bike fitter, be sure to mention that you intend to ride gravel, perhaps for many hours on end. This will inform the setup that your fitter recommends. Typically, you want a slightly more upright position on a gravel bike compared to a road bike. You need to be comfortable, ready to absorb the rough roads ahead.

Run whatcha brung: Almost any bike will work for Barry-Roubaix, depending on the skill of the rider.

Wheel and tire sizes

No discussion of gravel bike choices is complete without a close look at wheel and tire size. Once you commit to a bike, you also commit to its tire capabilities and limitations. This isn't a bad thing, but understanding the different wheel/tire platforms will help inform your bike-buying decision. There are three wheel sizes that you'll see when you begin to look at bikes that will work for gravel riding, whether you're planning to buy new or used. Because marketing people can't come to a consensus on what to call a given size, the choices can be confusing. When describing a rim, road bike companies will describe it in metric terms, while mountain bikers stick to imperial measurements. This is maddening, especially when they are describing the exact same dimension. Here's a quick guide to the conversion between road and mountain bike rims:

700C = 29 INCHES
This is by far the most common size on road bikes, cyclocross bikes, and gravel bikes. Using the same diameter rim, mountain

bike companies also use this size, calling it a "29er," the approximate overall diameter with a 2-inch tire.

650B = 27.5 INCHES
This is a wheel size used on randonneuring bikes from the 1950s and '60s. It was also used on many of the original mountain bikes. It has found new life in the mountain bike world as a middle ground between 29er and 26er bikes, virtually eliminating 26 inches as a modern mountain bike wheel size. Gravel riders have begun to experiment with the rim size, using tires 47 to 50 millimeters wide (a bit less than 2 inches).

26 INCHES
This is the traditional mountain bike tire size and what you'll find if you decide that a used mountain bike suits your needs best. Most new mountain bikes, however, use one of the two sizes listed above.

Not only is rim diameter important, but so too is rim width. As you explore options online or at your local bike shop, pay attention to the internal, or bead-to-bead, width of rims. This is listed as a numerical figure followed by a capital C, with 19C meaning that the internal width is 19 millimeters. The width of the rim will affect the shape of the tire, since the width of the tire

and its cross-sectional shape will change when it is mounted on a wider or narrower rim. Roughly speaking, as you increase the width of a rim 1 millimeter, the tire will grow 0.4 millimeters in width. All tire manufacturers publish guidelines for rim widths for the tires they sell.

The latest trend is toward both wider rims and wider tires, in pursuit of decreased rolling resistance (up to a point) and increased comfort. But tire and rim combinations are not limitless. Mounting a very wide tire on a narrow rim can lead to injury (a 2-inch mountain bike tire on a 15mm internal-width rim isn't advisable, for example). Similarly, you shouldn't attempt to install a 25mm tire on a rim with an internal width of 30mm.

Unfortunately, rim and tire manufacturers haven't gotten on the same page enough to produce hard-and-fast rules on which combinations are safe. The European Tyre and Rim Technical Organisation (ETRTO) makes a recommendation with its ISO 5775 standard for

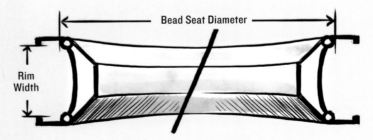

Bead seat diameter means "rim size," but that's just a starting point. The rolling diameter depends on tire choice, and rim width can affect tire profile dramatically.

RIM AND TIRE WIDTH COMPATIBILITY

TIRE WIDTH (MM)	RIM WIDTH (MM)								
	13C	15C	17C	19C	21C	23C	25C	27C	29C
18	✦								
20	✦								
23	✦	✦							
25	✦	✦	✦						
28		✦	✦	✦					
32		✦	✦	✦					
35			✦	✦	✦				
37			✦	✦	✦	✦			
40			✦	✦	✦	✦			
42				✦	✦	✦	✦		
44				✦	✦	✦	✦		
47				✦	✦	✦	✦	✦	
50				✦	✦	✦	✦	✦	
52				✦	✦	✦	✦	✦	✦
54					✦	✦	✦	✦	✦
57				✦	✦	✦	✦	✦	✦
60				✦	✦	✦	✦	✦	✦
62					✦	✦	✦	✦	✦

Adapted from Schwalbe Tires

labeling bicycle tires and rims. But its guidelines are outdated, with no recommendations for rims wider than 30C and tires larger than 2.5 inches. Mountain bike and gravel wheel and tire makers continue to push toward wider rims and tires, quickly surpassing 30C and 2.5 inches. When considering a given tire, it's best to refer to the manufacturer of the wheel in question. Many have recommendations on their websites. If not, reach out to them through the contact information on their websites to ensure that you're in safe territory.

Now that you understand rim diameters, we need to dig into tire size. You see, what matters most is how the pairing of a rim and a tire creates an overall diameter. For instance, putting a very wide tire on a given rim will increase the overall height or diameter of the combination versus using a narrower tire. While bikes that carry the label "gravel" will almost always have 700c wheels with tires in the 35 to 40mm range, more and more bike makers are playing with the idea of a smaller,

650b rim with even wider tires. Tires that measure 47 or 52mm wide mounted on this slightly smaller rim work on many existing framesets because the size moves the widest part of the tire lower in the fork and farther back in the frame. It's also convenient that 650b × 47mm equals in overall diameter a 700c × 28mm tire, so it doesn't affect gearing or bottom bracket height much. So, depending on your preferences, you may like the extra cushion of the wider 650b tire or the racier feel of the narrower 700c tire.

Similarly, on new mountain bikes, you may see 26+, 27.5+ (pronounced "twenty-seven-five-plus"), or 29+ wheels and tires listed. The "plus" in these cases denotes a wider than normal tire, typically in the 3-inch range, though recently the trend has been to pull it back a bit (2.6 or 2.8 inches). A 27.5+ (27.5 or 650b × 3.0 inches) wheel/tire is similar in size to a 29 × 2.1-inch wheel and tire. This allows a bike manufacturer to produce one frame and use it to create two very different

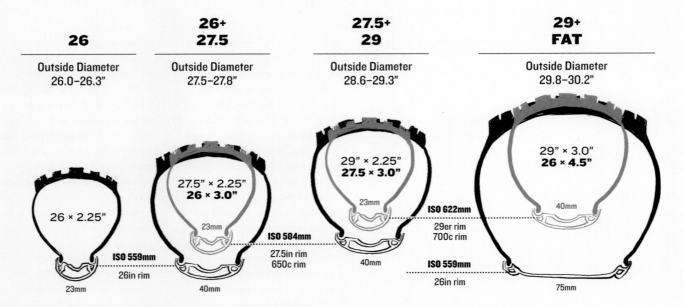

26

Outside Diameter
26.0–26.3"

26 × 2.25"

ISO 559mm

26in rim

23mm

26+
27.5

Outside Diameter
27.5–27.8"

27.5" × 2.25"
26 × 3.0"

23mm

ISO 584mm

27.5in rim
650c rim

40mm

27.5+
29

Outside Diameter
28.6–29.3"

29" × 2.25"
27.5 × 3.0"

23mm

40mm

29+
FAT

Outside Diameter
29.8–30.2"

29" × 3.0"
26 × 4.5"

40mm

ISO 622mm

29er rim
700c rim

ISO 559mm

26in rim

75mm

Equivalent diameters for four popular rim and tire combinations demonstrate the variety available today. Adapted from Jamis® Bikes.

bikes. It's a cost-saving measure, but one with real benefits for cyclists. However, keep in mind that while wider tires create additional traction and comfort, they are also heavier than narrower alternatives. It's a give-and-take that each rider has to weigh for him- or herself.

Here's a quick breakdown of common sizes for a given discipline. As you can see, lines often blur between disciplines:

ROAD

- 700c × 23–30mm

CYCLOCROSS

- 700c × 33mm is the widest allowed by the UCI (the race-sanctioning body), though amateurs can use larger sizes.

GRAVEL

Depending on the roads encountered and rider preference, all of the following are used:

- 700c × 28–45mm
- 29 × 2.1–2.2 inches
- 650b × 47mm

MOUNTAIN BIKE AND OFF-ROAD TOURING BIKES

- 26 × 2.2 inches
- 27.5 × 2.2–2.4 inches
- 29 × 2.0–2.4 inches

PLUS MOUNTAIN BIKE AND OFF-ROAD TOURING BIKES

- 26 × 2.8–3.0 inches
- 27.5 × 2.6–3.0 inches
- 29 × 2.6–3.0 inches

With the understanding that a bike that fits is far more important than the type of bike you ride, let's take a look at what options exist for gravel riders. All will work, but some will do so better than others.

Mountain bikes

The world is full of dusty, unridden mountain bikes that would love to be taken for a spin. Many high-quality used mountain bikes can be had for a song thanks to Craigslist and eBay. For gravel purposes, a bike with either a rigid fork or front suspension is what you'll need. For most riding, rear suspension isn't necessary, and maintaining it adds significantly to a bike shop tab.

Ideally, have a bike mechanic help you identify bikes that may work for you; if at all possible, have the mechanic accompany you when you meet with potential sellers (if the mechanic works in a shop, have the seller meet you there with the bike). The first item of business is to make sure the bike will fit you. After that, inspect the frame and fork for cracks, dents, and corrosion. Then move to the wheels. Are they round and straight? How about the drivetrain? Is it filthy or corroded? If so, you should look elsewhere, because a poorly maintained drivetrain is both a sign of a neglected bike and an expensive repair item. Least important are the tires, the pedals, the saddle, and other accessories such as a computer or water bottle cages. If they come with the bike, fine; they may work for you. For contact

A hardtail mountain bike (front suspension only) is an inexpensive way to try gravel cycling.

points, you'll likely need to experiment to find the right saddle, and you'll surely have your own preferences for pedals and tires.

A mountain bike can be an inexpensive way to try gravel road riding. But beware of bikes that have been abused. A dust-covered machine with little wear on the drivetrain is likely to have been used only lightly. On the other hand, a bike covered in dried mud and grease has been ridden hard and put away without maintenance, a warning sign of future problems.

Road bikes

In many parts of North America, a road bike can handle dirt roads as long as you take it easy when the going gets bumpy.

At some gravel races with smooth dirt surfaces, road bikes, though perhaps not the fastest way to cover the course, can get the job done. If you already own a road bike or have access to one, there is no reason you shouldn't head out the door and explore the roads less traveled in your backyard. Once you've done so, you'll have a better idea of your level of interest and what the roads in your area are like.

As the gravel category expands, manufacturers are increasingly blending the lines between road bike and dirt lane explorer. At the time of this writing, bikes like BMC's Roadmachine, Trek's Domane, Specialized's Diverge, Giant's Defy, and others like them are designed with rough

Road bikes are more capable than you might think. Put fatter tires on yours and give it a whirl.

roads in mind, and most of them will fit a 30 to 32mm tire.

If most of your cycling will be on paved roads with only occasional dirt sections, then a road bike may suit your needs best. They tend to be lighter than gravel bikes, with zippier handling to boot. But if your budget keeps you to one bike, the versatility of a dedicated gravel bike may be a better choice. Don't underestimate the roadworthiness of a gravel bike, especially if you spoon on a pair of smooth road tires when you are undertaking long paved rides.

If you're in an area with chunky gravel, it's best to shy away from a road bike if you want a bike that feels at home in the rough stuff. The bigger tires, longer wheelbase, and increased water-carrying capacity of a gravel bike do work better and will never hamstring you if you decide to travel to gravel events around the country.

Cyclocross bikes

Cyclocross, or 'cross, bikes are the go-to for many gravel riders. These highly capable, versatile machines are well suited to gravel riding thanks to generous tire clearance, robust framesets, low gearing, and brakes with good mud clearance. For many avid cyclists, if they could own only one bike it

would be a 'cross bike. A cyclocross bike will work well on paved roads, have room for fenders when pressed into service as a commuter, and will take on mild singletrack riding.

If you're already a cyclocross racer or planning a full 'cross campaign in the future with only limited gravel racing, then a 'cross bike is undoubtedly the way to go. Thankfully, many cyclocross bike makers are beginning to design their machines with ample tire clearance for tires wider than those commonly used for 'cross. This is helpful for racing in muddy conditions and for riders interested in trying a gravel race.

If you prefer a drop bar for your gravel riding but find yourself on a limited budget, you will find many used cyclocross bikes on the market. Again, if your technical expertise is limited, you may want to seek help in selecting one. A best-case scenario is finding a sponsored cyclocross racer who gets new bikes each season. The racer in this situation has to ride the latest equipment to promote his or her sponsors, setting aside a perfectly good bike that is well suited for gravel riding pursuits. This creates an opportunity for cash-strapped riders. Exploit it!

Gravel bikes

Many will contend that the difference between cyclocross bikes and gravel bikes is minimal, that the bike industry is splitting hairs in an attempt to sell more bikes. Well, I would argue differently.

Cyclocross bikes are great on gravel and versatile enough for road duty and light singletrack.

A cyclocross bike will certainly work for many people on many roads, but a gravel bike, with its increased tire clearance, more stable geometry, and shock-absorbing technologies, is more comfortable for the long haul than a bike that is designed for the 45- to 60-minute sprint effort that defines cyclocross. They are different, even if to the layperson's eye the differences are hard to spot.

The Union Cycliste Internationale (UCI) governs cyclocross racing at the top echelons of the sport. One rule for elite racers limits the width of tires to 33mm. Because of this, many cyclocross bikes are built solely with clearances for 33mm tires, plus a small allowance for some mud. But in cyclocross, you are allowed to exchange bikes during the race. For top pros, teams of mechanics grab the exchanged bike, wash off the mud, and ready it for yet another exchange. Over the course of a 60-minute race, a competitor may perform 20 or more exchanges. In other words, mud buildup is not a long-lasting hindrance.

Gravel racing, on the other hand, is designed with self-sufficiency as a founding principle. There is no follow car. There sometimes are checkpoints that allow for support, but in between those points, racers are on their own to face the challenges of the course and the elements. The rough nature of many of these roads is a far cry from the somewhat manicured courses of cyclocross races. Because of this, pioneering gravel racers began fitting the widest tires they could squeeze into the 'cross bikes they rode. Eventually, bike makers took note and began increasing tire clearance on the first true gravel bikes. Today, many gravel-specific bikes accept 40 to 45mm tires, with plenty of mud clearance.

Simultaneously, gravel bike makers also began to lower bottom brackets and lengthen wheelbases for extra stability. Gravel bikes are designed to prioritize stability so that less work is required to keep them rolling straight down loose gravel roads. Conversely, cyclocross courses are twisting, turning affairs where a highly nimble bike is an advantage. Steep frame angles, short wheelbases, and high bottom brackets help cyclocross bikes turn quickly.

Gravel bikes will typically come with disc brakes that offer good braking performance in adverse conditions. With long days in mind, a set of bosses for a third water bottle cage is often added to the underside of the down tube.

At the time of this book's publication, gravel bikes are offered with frames made from steel, aluminum, titanium, and carbon fiber. Influences for gravel bikes are diverse, with some companies rooted in the gravel scene while others bring experience from road and mountain

Dedicated gravel bikes are getting racier. This aerodynamic 3T Exploro is designed for speed.

bike development. Manufacturers such as 3T are experimenting with aerodynamic frame shapes, and racers have begun to use deep-section aero wheels for gravel races. Similarly, the bicycle industry has continued to blur the line between different categories, fitting 27.5-inch mountain bike wheels and 2-inch-wide tires to some gravel bikes (700 × 40mm and 27.5 × 2.0 inches are essentially the same diameter). It's an exciting time to enter the mixed-surface riding world. If you can dream it, someone is likely already offering your ideal bike.

With prices starting around $1,000 for new bikes and soaring into the price-tag stratosphere, options abound to suit all

wallets. When shopping for any new or used bike, be sure to budget for a few changes to the bike's saddle, stem, or handlebars. You'll also need a way to carry fluids and spares.

The finer points

While bike manufacturers are now producing bikes with gravel and dirt road riding specifically in mind, so too are some accessory makers. Once you have a bike that suits your needs, be sure to pay attention to the details that can make riding gravel a faster, more comfortable endeavor. From how you carry the fluids and calories you'll need for a day in the saddle to the

tires that serve as your connection to the road, here are some helpful tips on selecting the parts and accessories you use.

FUELING THE RIDE

If you ride in remote areas—and that's part of the point of seeking out gravel roads—you'll want to be sure that you can carry enough sports drink, water, and food to get you safely from point A to point B. Mid-ride stops are a perk to cycling long miles, so be sure to enjoy them. But also be certain that you plan well so that you don't suffer the dreaded *bonk*, a severe drop in blood sugar levels and a corresponding drop in energy. Dehydration is another danger. Both can be avoided with planning and preparation. Let's explore the question of drinks first, and then move on to carrying food.

STAYING HYDRATED

Most bikes can carry two water bottles, usually one on the seat tube and another on the down tube. For many rides, this will suffice, but once you start to venture out for longer jaunts, especially on hot days, you will quickly find that you need to carry more.

The first place many riders look to carry an extra bottle is in the back pocket of a cycling jersey. This is a good, simple solution for some. Try it before moving on to more expensive setups.

A hydration backpack is a great choice. With the capacity for 1.5 to 3 liters of water, a hydration pack also offers easy drinking thanks to an always-handy drink tube.

Joe Meiser | Salsa Cycles

GRAVEL BIKE DESIGN PIONEER

As a gravel racer, bikepacker, and product manager for Salsa Cycles, Joe Meiser has been instrumental in bringing several groundbreaking bikes to market. Meiser also oversees bags, parts, accessories, and clothing for Salsa while somehow making time to prepare and race in some of the hardest gravel events in the United States. He is also a past winner of the supremely difficult Trans Iowa and a finisher of the Tour Divide. Salsa's motto is Adventure by Bike, and over the past decade, the company has sponsored events and racers in an enthusiastic effort to enrich the worlds of gravel cycling and bikepacking.

"In 2009 and 2010, Salsa's motto 'Adventure by Bike' started to really gain a lot of use. Then fatbikes came."

Tell us about your background at Salsa Cycles and its involvement in gravel.

I started at Quality Bicycle Products [the parent company of Salsa] in 2004. When I came in, Surly was the prominent brand. Salsa was really struggling to find its way in the world. It had a lot of weird bikes—everything from cross-country bikes to a time trial bike at one point in time.

At the same time, Surly was really focused and successful. The first time I was introduced to gravel was via Surly. Surly used to run an ad that was that classic picture of a Minimum Maintenance road sign. You know, the mud, the field, and so on. It was a really vivid image that I had of that space. At the same time, I started taking notice of some of the history of the [Tour] Divide. In 2004, Mike Curiak first rode the Divide.

I was in this new environment and had always been, frankly, not great at short-format racing, like classic cross-country events. I didn't enjoy the experience of loading up the car every weekend and doing mediocre at a race. There was definitely something missing. Driving two hours there and back for only two hours on the bike didn't really jibe for me.

So I said to myself, "Shoot, I think I'll enter the Trans Iowa" [laughs]. I had done some smaller, local gravel events and some centuries on a road bike, but I'd never ridden more than 100 miles at a time before I did that event.

The first time I raced Trans Iowa was 2007, on a hardtail mountain bike with 2.1-inch tires, with flat bars and bar-ends. Midway through the race, I realized you didn't need that much bike. But that was the recommended equipment at the time. Ira Ryan showed up on one of his bikes and absolutely crushed it. [Ryan raced on a bike with 28mm tires and drop bars that year

Joe Meiser tries out one of his creations on singletrack.

and won. Meiser finished fifth.] It was pretty evident that a drop bar bike was the right vehicle for the event.

Meanwhile, we had been building disc cyclocross bikes for years. In 2004, Salsa had a disc cyclocross bike called the Las Cruces. In 2007, we launched the La Cruz, which was a steel drop bar cyclocross bike that fit up to a 42mm tire. Jason Boucher [brand manager], Mike Reimer [marketing manager], a few others, and I were riding those and constantly stuffing the biggest tires we could into them. It was really fun. We could ride singletrack and mixed surface.

So the Fargo evolved out of that experimentation?
Yes. Around that time, we asked ourselves, "What if we designed a dirt drop 29er? There seems to be this pent-up demand with what's going on in gravel, with Divide racing, with monster 'cross." So we did that.

After I did well at Trans Iowa, I had been loosely planning on racing the Divide. So when we wrote the brief for designing the Fargo, we said we were going to design the best bike for what we thought racing the Divide would look like. We immediately gravitated toward drop bars because of all the hand problems that people would report. Look back at those early reports of Divide racing; the biggest problems were hand and wrist related. People were trying to overcome it by double- and triple-wrapping bars, running aerobars and bar-ends. That was a problem that we could solve.

The other part was how you carry the gear. Bikepacking was coming about at the time. Revelate Designs was young then as a brand. Eric Parsons had some pretty interesting and really novel solutions. So Boucher and I got onto his waiting list to get a feedbag, a handlebar harness, and a frame pack for those

The Salsa Fargo was an early stab at a dirt drop 29er design.

prototype Fargos. We wanted to try that methodology out. It was still very early.

The Fargo launched in fall 2008. It was a steel dirt drop 29er. At the same time, you can look back and see that dirt drop handlebars, part of the monster 'cross genre, part of gravel, were heavily sought after. You could find a Nitto-made WTB dirt drop on eBay going for an exorbitant amount of money for what it cost to produce that bar.

It was pretty evident that the market wanted a dirt drop again. So we started down that path with the Woodchipper. Now it's a pretty iconic bar. We still do quite well with it, even though we've introduced the Cowbell and the Cowchipper.

How did the bike perform on Tour Divide?
In general, I was satisfied. That first Fargo was a strange bike. It was designed to be a 29er dirt drop bike/loaded touring bike. It had a full set of rack and fender mounts. That said, by

today's standards, the handling would be terrible. It had a really long rear end, 460mm. We were trying to fit a triple with a 2.4-inch tire. The options we had were slim. The front end of the bike, with the drop bar, we did not get the handling right. We didn't have a good handle on how people would ride it and how they would load it. It had really light front-end handling and shimmy, depending on where you put the load on the bike. It was weird for sure.

The fork had triple mounts on the legs to increase water-carrying possibilities. Right about then was when people were using hose clamps to mount extra cages. The third hole on our fork wasn't spaced equally from the other two. It was for bolting on a bungee strap to help keep the bottle from flying out. We never expected it [to be used] for cargo. It was on the next generation that we spaced them evenly and started looking at the Anything Cage. On some sizes, you could run six water bottles.

What was the genesis of the Warbird?
We were seeing gravel grow out of the Midwest. Gravel racing did exist before the 2000s, but only later did we see it grow into its current definition. We were not doing well with cyclocross bikes because we weren't a 'cross brand. We were a racing brand. At that point, we still weren't Adventure by Bike, but we didn't do well with traditional bike models.

But we were doing really well with the Fargo. We had it leading us in terms of brand. With the cyclocross bikes coming up for a redesign, someone floated the idea of designing a bike for gravel. With that question, a very different set of parameters evolved. It wasn't drastic at the time, but we tweaked the geometry. A little bit longer wheelbase, certainly more tire clearance, a little lower bottom bracket because you

The Warbird was among the first production gravel bikes.

didn't have the off-camber 180-degree turns of cyclocross. We made it a bit more compliant because you were going to be on it for hours, not one hour.

We launched the Warbird in 2011 or '12, the first modern production gravel bike. That was pretty polarizing. A lot of people thought that there wasn't a difference between it and a 'cross bike. But it was authentic to what we were doing. And we were out racing it in 2009, 2010, and beyond. I raced Trans Iowa on a prototype of it in 2010 and 2011. The first Warbird was offered in aluminum and titanium. Carbon models came later, in 2015. That bike leads the way for us. We're now on the fourth generation of the Warbird.

The Fargo is still in the line, but now the Cutthroat, launched in June 2015, is a bike that redefined what we think the best Tour Divide bike is. While it was designed as a bikepacking racer bike, we consistently see them show up at gravel races.

For Land Run, it's really popular, in part because of the mud clearance and in part because of how it rides.

Can you tell us about Salsa's take on adventure?

Just before I did the Divide on the Fargo, in 2009, *National Geographic* called riding the Divide one of their bucket list items. That helped give Salsa a focus.

In 2009 and 2010, Salsa's motto Adventure by Bike started to really gain a lot of use. Then fatbikes came. Full-suspension bikes came. Evolutions came. Titanium. Additional handlebars, et cetera all came out of that time period.

Now, seven years later, we've really helped define what adventure means to cyclists. It has really fragmented. We have several gravel bikes now, just like some brands have several road bikes. It's a bit absurd, but it's also really cool.

Which accessories have changed the gravel and bikepacking game?

Wider-range road drivetrains have come about. Disc brakes have become commonplace. When we first started riding gravel early on, the biggest liability was mud packing up in your cantis [cantilever brakes]. It was a big challenge.

Tires were another important area. Until two years ago, options were pretty dismal. You might have found a tire that worked well for a specific segment, but the manufacturer changed it because it was a cross-country or cyclocross race tire. Then the casing changes, and it's no longer as durable, or the rubber compound changes, and it won't last for 200 miles of gravel. Now there are brands launching good gravel-specific tires. The trend to wider road rims is great. Those have really improved the component selection.

The most important thing for bikepacking and gravel is the rackless touring and bikepacking bags. Eric at Revelate is one of the most important people in the space. He really changed what was possible on a bike, because all of a sudden, how you carried stuff wasn't a liability. You can look back at early reports of bikepacking and Divide riders, and one of the biggest liabilities was racks. Even with a rack with a dry bag on top, it is still held on with an M5 bolt. It's rattling down a dirt road for hundreds of miles. Guess what? It rattles loose and falls out. Welds on the racks fail; tubing fails. Mounting systems for panniers on racks fail. Then Eric comes in and commercializes [bikepacking bags], making them broadly available. Beforehand, you had Carousel Design Works, Jeff Boatman, who did something similar early on. But he never really ramped up production.

Eric was the first to come along with custom full-frame bags, seat bags, and handlebar mounting solutions. He had top tube bags and the Jerrycan concept. The Tangle bag, a half frame bag with a reservoir inside, was really important for gravel for many years. For me, that meant that I was able to complete half of Trans Iowa, or 150 miles, without stopping at a gas station. Checkpoints are time sucks. You don't necessarily have to ride extremely fast. That always helps. But consistency is probably more important than speed. If you're focused on short transitions or eliminating them, you are effectively faster.

Hands down, those products are the most important thing. Outside the bike industry was a trend in ultralight backpacking. Guys like Andrew Skurka doing superfast, light big treks. Roman Dial doing big trips with minimalist kits. Sleeping kits became lighter. Clothing became lighter. You can move faster because you're carrying less.

What's on the horizon for adventure riders?

Segmentation. If you look at our line, we have the Fargo, the Cutthroat, the Vaya, and the Warbird. Those are basically four different takes on bikes for mixed-surface terrain. I don't see that changing.

There is room to make new parts and accessories. Is there room for more handlebars? Is there room for other ways to improve rider comfort and efficiency? The same thing is true of bags. As a rider, I used to run a Tangle bag in gravel races. Now I don't. How am I solving those problems differently? There is a ton of room in parts and accessories, particularly around soft goods.

For the bikepacking piece, the biggest opportunity is education. That's a big challenge that first go-round. It seems to be a monumental task: Okay, I'm going to put all this on there and ride over there, camp, and then ride back? I don't think we can underestimate the challenge of that. We can't diminish how hard that is. It's a big barrier.

In terms of where bikepacking goes, a bikepacking bike for off-road use is a mountain bike. There can be design features of the bike, like the large front triangle on the Woodsmoke, to make room for a larger frame bag. But it's a mountain bike at its core.

But in general, in the last few years, I've loved the new drivetrains and tires and wheels. All of these things present new possibilities for putting together elements to create interesting, new ride vehicles. I'm fortunate to be at a place that encourages that and is willing to invest in that, the weird and wacky.

A dirt drop 29er is kind of absurd if you think about it, but our leadership believed in it. They said, "Sure, we'll let you guys do that. If you believe in it, we believe in you." And that's pretty cool.

Water everywhere: There are plenty of places for cages if you get creative.

Bikepacking bags can fit around your bottles, and also serve to hold reservoirs.

Even on rough roads, it's a simple matter to quickly get the tube to your mouth and then return your hand to the bars. This makes staying hydrated when riding in loose gravel much more convenient. But there are two downsides to hydration packs: They can be hot, and their added weight increases the pressure of your derriere against the saddle. Regulating your heat with wardrobe changes is also a bit slower, as you will need to take off the pack to remove a jacket or vest as a day warms up.

Adding additional water bottle carriers to your bike is another solution. If your bike doesn't have a third set of bottle cage mounts on the underside of the down tube, you can simply tape a cage to the frame. You'll want to check first to see if a bottle will safely clear the front tire. If it does, then use electrical tape to cover the frame where the cage will make contact. This is to protect the frame's finish. Then use additional tape, wrapping the frame and threading it through the cage, to secure your new carrier. This works best with cages that are fairly open. Salsa's Nickless cage is a great choice for this trick.

Another increasingly popular location for extra cages is on the outside of the fork legs. Some bikes, especially those designed with bikepacking in mind, come with threaded inserts in the legs. If your bike is without these, a combination of tape and hose clamps (on metal fork legs only—not carbon!) can be used to mount a set of cages. Be sure to experiment with this

Hydration packs are convenient and commodious.

Bikepacking bags that mount to your bicycle are an option that is gaining popularity in gravel circles. They are a light, convenient way to carry extra gear, whether in clothing, spares, food, or water. Frame bags or partial frame bags that are strapped to the inside of a bike's main triangle can easily carry an extra water bottle or the reservoir from a hydration pack. Revelate Designs's Tangle bag is one such product that works with many different bikes.

Handlebar bags, many of which mount beside the stem, offer a very convenient location for extra water bottles. JPaks's RukSak is a cylindrical bag that straps to the handlebar, stem, and fork crown to securely carry up to a 1-liter bottle, even over rough terrain. Many bikepacking bag makers offer something similar. Using one or a pair of these is a great way to carry extra fluids.

FEED THE MONSTER

Food is easier to carry than water because it is much denser. Carrying a variety of foods is a good idea, particularly on long days. Energy bars, gels, and gummies are a good start. But adding a banana, a small sandwich, or other real food can make the thought of eating more attractive. Don't be afraid to experiment; food and cycling have a direct correlation. Put in good-quality fuel, and the result is a good-quality ride. Gobble down junk food, and you're likely to suffer.

Jersey pockets are the first place to stash your favorite ride fuel. Doing so doesn't noticeably add weight to the rider/

Extra credit gravel trick

If carrying a bottle down low, either on the underside of the down tube or on the fork, cover the drink nozzle with a plastic sandwich bag and a rubber band. This will keep it free of mud and manure, keeping you healthier.

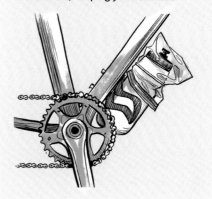

bike combination if you usually ride in a cycling jersey. If you go this route, mentally organizing your pockets can be helpful. For instance, put your gels in one pocket, solid food in another, and store trash in the third pocket.

If your pockets are already carrying your wallet, cell phone, or perhaps some extra clothing, there are great ways to put your food on your bike. Triathlon is again an inspiration, with gravel riders using so-called bento boxes on the top tubes of their bikes. These mount behind the stem and keep your food easily accessible. Some riders

setup before relying on it for a race. It takes practice to safely grab bottles from a fork leg while pedaling down the road.

If you use aerobars, you can use a triathlon-style bottle cage that mounts between the aerobar extensions. This keeps a bottle handy and also acts as a visual reminder to drink. Another tri trick: some gravel riders have luck mounting extra cages behind their saddle. If you go this route, be sure to spend the extra money on cages that grip the bottles tightly. Otherwise, these behind-the-saddle cages can easily eject bottles, leaving you dry and thirsty.

instead use these to carry their wallet and phone, preferring to keep food in their jersey. This is an entirely personal preference.

Bikepacking bag makers offer top tube bags that are typically larger than those aimed at triathletes. If you find yourself needing more room for storage, check out Revelate's Gas Tank, Blackburn's Outpost, Apidura's Top Tube Pack, or Alpkit's Fuel Pods. These and other products work extremely well. You can even order custom colored bags from many makers.

Likewise, the frame and partial frame bags mentioned earlier are a great way to carry extra food. Most are quite easy to open with one hand while riding. If you prefer, you can also use a frame bag to free up your jersey pockets for food, putting your clothing, phone, and wallet in the bag.

If you only need to carry a number of extra energy gels, simply tape them to your stem or top tube. Align the top of the gel so that it remains taped to the bike, and simply tear off the gel to eat it.

Ultimately, there is no single solution for carrying food and drink that is right for every rider on every ride. You'll need to see what's best for you based on how much you need to eat and drink, as well as the roads that you like to ride. Speak with your fellow gravel riders about their preferences. Borrow a bag from a friend before you buy, if possible. None of the choices mentioned here break the bank, but trying every one of them would become expensive. That said, if you decide to take on gravel races or simply challenge yourself with long rides, you may come up with several solutions that work for you, depending on the ride you have in mind. That's all part of the fun.

Bits and bobs

Now that you're assured that you're able to carry enough fuel to keep your engine running, let's turn our focus to the parts that make a bike more capable on gravel. Although many bikes come with excellent equipment straight out of the box, small changes may suit your needs even better. In many cases, you can simply improve your bike as the components wear out. In other situations—gearing, for instance—you may need to make changes immediately to ensure that you can complete the rides you have in mind.

TIRES

Here's the thing: Punctures stink. They're no fun. I always advise riders who are researching new gravel tires to err on the side of heft. Sure, thicker tires will be a little slower on the hills, but you'll be riding up the hills instead of mumbling curse words while parked on the side of the road after your third flat of the day.

For most gravel road surfaces, you don't need a very aggressive tread pattern. Mountain bike tires certainly work. If they give you added confidence and your bike has room for them, go that route. But if you're interested in getting down the road a bit more quickly, look for a tread that has a smooth center section and small knobs along the sides for stability and cornering.

In the past, gravel riders used cyclocross and touring tires to explore rural areas. Both had good points, and some riders continue to favor them, but recently a slew of tires made specifically for gravel riders have become available. With sizes from 28 to 50mm and a wide variety of tread patterns, there's never been a better time to look at gravel tires. Most of them are also designed to run without inner tubes. A tubeless setup is a great way to avoid punctures, save weight, and decrease rolling resistance.

Derived from mountain bike tire technology, tubeless tires help eliminate pinch flats, a puncture where the tube is pinched between the rim and a road obstacle. With the use of a liquid latex tubeless sealant, small punctures from thorns or glass are often sealed without the rider ever knowing there was a problem.

Stan Koziatek, in 2001, was the first to commercially produce a tubeless sealant for cycling. That product has

---

Extra credit gravel trick

Open the wrappers on your energy bars before you head out on your ride. It makes eating on the fly a little bit easier and incentivizes you to finish all the food you're carrying.

Tubeless installation tips

1 INSTALL THE RIM STRIP.
Ensure that it covers all the spoke
holes and completely covers
the rim's internal bed. Don't
install the tubeless valve yet.

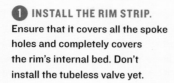

**2 INSTALL THE TIRE WITH AN
INNER TUBE.** Use a conventional
inner tube, and install by hand if
possible. Pump it up and ensure
the tire seats on both sides. Let it
sit for a few hours to stretch out
the bead, to make reseating the
tire easier in the next steps. Then
deflate the tube and remove it,
being careful to disturb only one
side of the tire's bead. Leaving
the other side of the tire fully
seated will help you greatly.

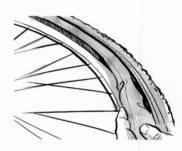

**3 INSTALL THE TUBELESS
VALVE.** Always use a tubeless
valve with a removable Presta
valve core. With the valve
in place, lever the half of
the tire you unseated back
into the rim's spoke bed.

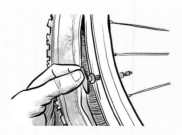

4 SEAT THE TIRE. Before
adding any sealant, use your pump
to try to seat the tire bead. This is
where a compressor is helpful. If
the tire won't seat, use a tire lever
to move the tire bead into position
against the rim's edge. Do this as
far around as you can. Then try to
inflate the tire again. With trial and
error, it will eventually seat fully.

5 UNSCREW THE VALVE CORE.
Once the tire is seated, remove
the valve core from the tubeless
valve. Using a hose or injector
(supplied by the sealant maker),
inject the prescribed amount of
sealant into the tire. Wipe off any
excess and reinstall the valve core.

6 PUMP UP THE TIRE. If you
hear air escaping, rotate the tire to
put that point at the bottom of the
wheel. Shake the wheel/tire. The
air will force sealant into the void,
sealing the leak. Pretty cool, eh?

evolved over the years and is now known as Stan's NoTubes. Others have joined the sealant scene, with Orange Seal, Hutchinson, Bontrager, Slime, Schwalbe, Effetto Mariposa, and Vittoria all selling variations. Several of these manufacturers produce multiple types of sealant designed specifically for cold weather riding, racing, or durability. Orange Seal's Endurance formula is made to last a long time and works well in arid climates. All of these sealants use liquid latex or something similar, and small particulates (think glitter) suspended in a solution. Over time, that solution can evaporate, so it's important that you regularly check the sealant level in your tires.

Running tubeless tires requires tubeless-compatible rims as well, but many rims sold on gravel and cyclocross bikes are ready to go once the appropriate rim strips and valves are installed. The initial setup of a tubeless system can be frustrating, especially when it comes to pumping enough air into the tires quickly enough to seat the tire beads against the rim. This task is best done using an air compressor or one of the new breed of floor pumps that have a compression chamber. But as you read reviews of new tires online, the reviewer will often mention whether setup is possible using a normal floor pump. For my own preferred method to wrangle these tires into place, see the sidebar "Tubeless installation tips."

If you experience a puncture while riding, first try to add air to your setup. Both carbon dioxide cartridges and pumps will work for this. In many cases, the additional air will force sealant to the hole. Typically, the escaping sealant helps you locate the cause of the puncture. If you find a thorn or small piece of wire, leave it in place. The objective at this point is to get home or to the finish line. You can remove the offending object later. If the puncture was caused by a sharp rock or shard of glass, however, it's often best to remove it, as it can otherwise continue to open up the hole in the tire as you ride.

If the hole won't seal using the sealant and extra air, you will need to install a tubeless plug or a spare tube. In this case, be sure to remove whatever caused the puncture. A plug won't work next to a foreign object, and if installing a tube, you don't want the sharp offender to puncture

Tread patterns from left: knobby, semi-slick, file. Note that most file treads aren't truly smooth, with vestigial knobs for traction in fine gravel. Semi-slicks are more popular.

your spare. You'll also need to remove the tubeless valve before installing the tube. Be sure to keep track of the tubeless valve during this process. You'll want it once you install a new tire, or after patching the tubeless tire with a tubeless patch.

For further tubeless tips, ask your local shop for details and a demonstration. Shops that sell gravel bikes regularly will have plenty of experience in making tubeless systems work flawlessly.

Regarding tires, there are essentially three tread patterns that are gravel appropriate: knobby, slick, and hybrid. A full knobby is the most aggressive. Essentially mini–mountain bike tires, knobbies such as WTB's Nano 40 or Bruce Gordon's Rock 'n Road are capable of handling singletrack as well as deep sand and loose gravel. These tires will get you through the sketchiest of sections and are great for riders who lack confidence in loose conditions. The trade-off is a heavier tire that is a bit slower on smooth surfaces.

A full slick, or essentially smooth tire, is great for riders who see more tarmac and prioritize low rolling resistance over stability in technical situations. Some tires in this category will have mild herringbone patterns or a series of small knobs to add traction, but the overall surface is consistent. Schwalbe's G-One, Compass's Bon Jon Pass, and Clement's USH 32 are tubeless tires with very little tread that offer a fast, responsive ride on smooth roads and hard-packed dirt.

Extra credit gravel trick

Check your tubeless tire sealant several times a year to ensure that it hasn't evaporated or been used up sealing previous small punctures. Also, carry a small tire plug kit with your spares. Installing a plug is faster than putting in a tube and generally works well for everything except large cuts and sidewall tears.

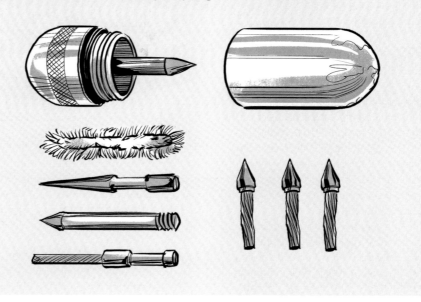

The third tread pattern is perhaps the most popular. It is a hybrid of the knobby and the slick, using a fast-rolling, smooth center section flanked by a series of side knobs for stability in loose conditions and cornering traction. Specialized's Trigger, Teravail's Cannonball, Clement's MSO, WTB's Riddler, and Panaracer's GravelKing SK are excellent examples. In most cases, a gravel rider, whether seasoned or novice, will be most comfortable on a semi-slick or hybrid tire simply because it will work well in virtually all conditions.

Tire selection involves more than just tread pattern, though. Tire size and construction also play a significant factor. A larger tire will be more comfortable and offer better handling in most conditions. But be sure not to go too far with width if the forecast looks like rain. Narrower tires allow more room for mud in your frame and fork. When considering new tires, be sure to measure the clearances between the tire and the bike frame and fork. Several of the tires mentioned above are quite large and won't fit all bikes.

Tire size is also affected by rim width. Recently, many wheel makers have begun to increase the width of their rims to help support the sidewalls of wider tires. Running a 40mm tire on a very narrow rim can actually be dangerous at extremely low pressures. The sidewall of the tire can begin to fold under pressure from cornering and unseat the bead of the tire inside the rim, causing what many call a "burp." This can lead to deflation and a loss of control. Even if your bike has room for larger tires, be sure that the rims are up to the task of supporting your tire of choice.

The interplay between tire and rim width means you can experiment with a narrower tire on a wider rim, with the rim effectively making the tire wider without added tire weight. The trade-off is that there is less tire between potential puncture-inducing rocks and the rim; the upside is less weight and slightly quicker handling.

The construction of the tire is also important. A heavier tire should theoretically be more puncture resistant. Manufacturers use layers of nylon and Kevlar fabric in tires to help prevent flats. Depending on where you ride, a lighter, more supple tire will save weight and roll a tad faster. The gravel in Iowa and Nebraska

CO_2 inflators are small and convenient, but they're a one-shot proposition.

is typically smooth, and a light tire shines in those conditions. On the other hand, if you're heading to the Flint Hills of Kansas for the Dirty Kanza, you'll want a very robust tire.

CARRY-ALONG INFLATION OPTIONS

Flat tires do happen. Not often, we hope, but it's best to plan for them. The choice on what to carry as you pedal back roads comes down to two options: pumps and CO_2 inflators. Both have their advantages.

Pumps will inflate as long as you have the strength to use them. The downside is that pumping up a tire can take some time, especially with large-volume tires. Thankfully, both frame pumps and mini-pumps have improved in recent years. Lezyne produces some durable mini-pumps that fit in a jersey pocket or mount

to a bicycle using a Velcro strap and clip bolted between the frame and a water bottle cage. Some of them even have integrated pressure gauges.

For multiday adventures, Lezyne, Blackburn, and Topeak all make what is essentially a small, portable floor pump. This adds a bit of weight and bulk to your gear, but for daily top-offs, they are much more effective than hand pumps.

The venerable Italian pump company Silca has begun producing very high quality frame pumps in the United States. These are typically carried on the underside of the top tube and secured using a Velcro strap if the bike does not have carrying tabs. Thanks to the use of top-notch materials and a smart, fully serviceable design, a Silca frame pump should last a lifetime.

For race day situations or times when you want to inflate a tire quickly, a carbon dioxide (CO_2) inflator is the way to go. These inflators use compressed CO_2 cartridges designed for air pistols. You can find replacement cartridges at sporting goods stores and bike shops. The cartridges come in several different sizes to match the volume of your tires. The 12-gram cartridges are best for road bikes, 16- and 20-gram for cyclocross and gravel tires, and larger "Big Air" 40-gram canisters are handy for mountain bike tires.

Because the compressed CO_2 gets used up quickly, you generally need a cartridge for each puncture you encounter, which means packing some spares on each ride.

If you think you'll experience a lot of flats, or if you are on a multiday trip, you may want to carry a pump as a backup. Genuine Innovations, Planet Bike, MSW, Birzman, and others make cartridges of various sizes, though MSW is currently the only one making the 40-gram canisters. Silca, Lezyne, SKS, and the aforementioned cartridge makers all produce inflator heads.

GEARING

The gearing on a gravel bike is as personal as saddle choice. Some people like to spin a low gear, while others muscle their way through. But in general, speeds are lower in gravel riding. It's inherent in the surface. That surface also means that violent Tour de France–inspired sprinting is hard to do. Pedal strokes need to be smooth to avoid a loss of traction, especially when climbing. For this reason, many gravel riders prefer especially low climbing gears, sometimes with a 1:1 ratio or lower (for example, a 34-tooth small chainring and a 34-tooth large rear cog). This allows them to remain seated on climbs to maintain traction.

When looking at gearing, don't be too focused on the number of cogs across a cassette; 11-speed is not inherently better than 10-speed, or even 9-speed for that matter. In fact, in muddy conditions an 11-speed cassette can clog more quickly than one with more room between cogs. More important is to ensure that the largest cog and the smallest chainring

provide you with an appropriately easy low gear. The other end of the spectrum isn't as important, again because speeds are typically lower on gravel.

Your abilities, the roads you ride, and even the wheel size of your bike will all factor into your gearing equation. To begin with, go out and try what you have. If you're walking up every incline, consider a change. If you never use your lowest gear, you could lose a bit of bike weight and go with a stouter set of gears. In that case, though, I would suggest wearing out what you have on your bike first. No need to spend drivetrain money prematurely.

The most popular gearing setup on gravel bikes is a compact road crank with a 50-tooth large chainring and a 34-tooth small ring. Sometimes gravel bikes arrive with 46/36 rings. Both are good choices. Cassettes range from 11–25 to 11–32.

High-quality parts from Shimano, SRAM, and Campagnolo all work well for gravel shifting duties. Very recently, crank makers have begun to offer gravel-specific gearing. These cranks use a smaller spider to allow the use of 46/30 and 44/28 chainrings, which work well for gravel and are lighter than larger rings.

The advent of wide-ratio cassettes and chainrings with contoured teeth that retain a chain over bumpy ground led SRAM to encourage the use of a single chainring drivetrain. Many riders also build Shimano-equipped bikes using this 1× (pronounced "one by") type of drivetrain. Many gravel bike manufacturers are on board, selling bikes with 1×11 drivetrains. The upside is a lighter bike, thanks to the elimination of a second (and third) chainring, a front derailleur, and a front shifter. Many riders also prefer the simplicity of only thinking

Pie-plate-size cogs and wide-range derailleurs make 1× gearing highly capable.

in terms of easier or harder when shifting. The downside is a potential lack of range if the chosen cassette and chainring aren't adequate for a given rider or course.

For the ultimate in drivetrain simplicity, many gravel riders swear by a single speed setup. This saves weight and eliminates the maintenance duties of two shifters, two derailleurs, and two cables. In muddy gravel conditions that can devour a rear derailleur, single speed riders are all smiles. The downside is finding an optimal gear choice that matches your fitness, riding style, and the elevation profile of where you'll be riding. But if you're feeling strong, single speeding can be a lot of fun.

BRAKES

Just as important as the gears used to power a gravel bike are the brakes used to stop it. With dust, mud, water crossings, rain, and snow in a gravel bike's daily duties, there are few things that matter more than reliable braking. Because of these considerations, most of the gravel bikes sold today have disc brakes that offer excellent modulation in virtually all conditions and better mud clearance between the wheel and the frame. Discs also have the advantage of not using the rim as a braking surface, so that a rider can continue even if his wheel is slightly out of true. The drawbacks of disc brakes are that they are slightly heavier than rim brakes and may not be as easy to maintain.

Disc brakes, whether hydraulic or cable, have superior performance in all conditions.

There are two types of disc brakes: hydraulic and mechanical. Hydraulic brakes are actuated through fluid. As with a car or motorcycle, the brake lines must be bled of air periodically. You also cannot mix and match brands; bicycle disc brakes are closed systems requiring specific levers, hoses, and calipers. Shimano and SRAM are examples of hydraulic systems that work exceptionally well but are completely incompatible. Upsides to hydraulic brakes lie in their greater stopping power over mechanical brakes and the fact that the brake pads automatically adjust inward as they wear.

Mechanical disc brakes are actuated by a cable that runs through a housing. They are generally simple to work on, and mixing levers and calipers is rarely an

issue. However, cable brakes don't usually offer the same stopping power as hydraulic systems. Additionally, you need to adjust them as the pads wear. Avid, Shimano, TRP, and Paul Component all offer mechanical discs that work with drop bar brake levers.

Rim brakes (caliper brakes) still have lots to offer. They are easy to work on, lighter than disc brakes, and allow the use of older rim brake wheels as you build up a gravel arsenal. They're also easier to live with if you have many sets of wheels for one bike; with disc brakes, you must fiddle with the discs and hubs to make sure the lateral spacing of the disc is exactly the same on each wheel, unless you enjoy realigning the calipers each time you make a swap.

Rim brakes can be found on used bikes, as well as on some cyclocross and handmade frames. Cantilever or linear-pull brakes are made for drop bar and flat bar brake levers; some levers can work with both types of brakes. As pads wear, it's important to readjust these brakes. It's also vital to maintain the wheels, keeping them round and true, and to pay attention to braking surface wear.

Maintenance

Just a quick note on bicycle maintenance: A bicycle is a wonderful machine, simple in nature but often complex in practice. Performing maintenance on your bike is a good way to forestall problems that might otherwise arise while riding. But as bicycles continue to use lighter materials

Extra credit gravel trick

Fashion a portable mud scraper from a shish kebab skewer, a paint stirrer, or a tent stake. Use it to clear mud from the cassette, chainrings, pedals, tires, and your shoes.

and new technologies, educating yourself on the technical aspects of cycling becomes more involved. For example, a new carbon fiber handlebar is a nice upgrade, but if it isn't installed properly you risk serious injury if it breaks. When in doubt, seek help. There's no need to save a few bucks but ruin a ride in the process.

DAILY RIDE CHECKLIST

If you keep your bike in good working order, roadside problems are likely a rarity for you. Nonetheless, whenever you venture out on gravel roads, things can go wrong.

Punctures, broken chains, skipping gears, and loosening bolts are common gravel gremlins. With an emphasis on self-reliance, gravel riding encourages us to prepare for these eventualities. Carrying spares when heading out on gravel roads is a necessity. Here is a proposed list of what else to take along. Your list may be shorter or longer, depending on the level of risk you're willing to assume.

If you have all these items, you're off to a great start. If you have them but don't know how to use them, ask your local shop for some one-on-one time, and consider picking up Lennard Zinn's book *Zinn and the Art of Road Bike Maintenance*.

FOR EACH RIDE

- Water
- Food
- GPS
- Map of the area if you're in a new place
- Two spare inner tubes
- Patch kit and tire plug kit
- Tire levers
- Pump (can be supplemented with CO_2 inflator and cartridges)
- Multi-tool with chain tool
- Chain lube
- Chain quick link
- Derailleur hanger
- Zip ties and a length of duct tape (rolled around your pump)
- Wallet with ID, cash, and credit card
- Phone, with In Case of Emergency (ICE) contact saved
- Front and rear blinking lights

There's no better way to see the world than through the lens of your own bikepacking adventure.

⑦ BIKEPACKING GEAR FOR MULTIDAY ADVENTURES

In many cases, you can use the gravel bike you already own for overnight jaunts. The beauty of short overnight trips, coined "sub-24-hour overnighters" or "S24O" by Grant Petersen of Rivendell fame, is that you can experiment with various means of carrying your gear as well as different shelter options with only limited consequences. The longest you'll have to endure discomfort is one night. Once you're back home, you can take note of items that didn't work and adjust.

There are some changes to your bike that you may want to consider if you find yourself interested in bike camping or bikepacking. Even when hotels are used for lodging, most cyclists will carry extra clothing in case of poor weather and additional spares when leaving for a weeklong gravel ride. Carrying camping gear adds even more weight to your bike, as do cooking items and additional food. (We'll discuss how to carry these items in a little bit.)

Because of this additional heft, lower gears, better brakes, and wider tires can be useful bike modifications for multiday rides. Smaller gears save strain on knees, allowing riders to climb grades in relative comfort, spinning as they ascend. If possible, simply install a cassette with a larger cog (you may also need to lengthen the chain a few links). Smaller chainrings also help, though they should be changed only after exploring cassette options.

Traveling light makes bikepacking more fun. You may be surprised by how little gear you truly need out there.

Generally speaking, a one-tooth change in a rear cog equals a two-tooth change in a chainring. Cassettes and chains are also typically less expensive than a new crankset or chainrings. If you're running a 1× drivetrain on your gravel bike (see Chapter 6), install a smaller chainring and the largest cassette that the rear derailleur can handle. Ask your local bike shop if you can upgrade without buying a new derailleur.

Once you've crested those low-gear climbs, you may need additional stopping power on the other side to keep your loaded bike under control. This is where disc brakes shine. If you already have disc brakes and find power wanting, installing larger brake rotors and the associated caliper adapter will increase stopping power. But be sure to check with the bike manufacturer before you go overboard with rotor size. There are limits. In any case, few things are scarier than a runaway bike, so it's best to head out for a few test rides aboard your loaded bicycle before undertaking your first extended tour.

Wider tires disperse the load over a greater contact patch, decreasing the likelihood of punctures as well as adding traction and comfort. If you're not already taking maximum advantage of the tire clearance in your bike's frame and fork, you may want to consider it for bikepacking. The caveat is if you're expecting mud. Shoehorning the widest tire possible inside a frame and fork doesn't give built-up mud a

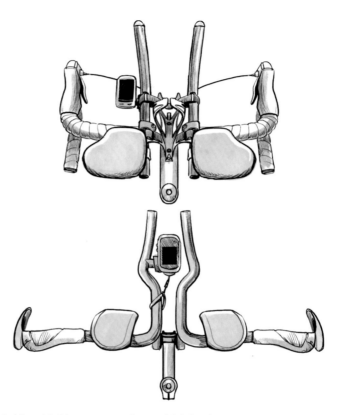

Aerobars, adapted from triathlon, are more about multiple hand positions than cheating the wind. They work with drop bars and flat bars.

place to go, quickly rendering it impossible for wheels to turn.

Although single-day racers may consider aerodynamics when setting up their bikes and therefore stick with a narrow handlebar, a wider bar offers more leverage to handle a loaded bicycle. It also opens up the chest to help ease breathing.

Aerobars are also popular with long-distance riders, whether on the road or gravel. This has more to do with relieving pressure on the hands than with aerodynamics. When installing an aerobar, it's advisable to keep it high and wide to help maintain control of the bike and to aid in breathing.

As bikepacking rigs evolve, they offer new and better ways to carry gear.

If you find that changes to your existing bike aren't sufficient for the rides you're attempting, you may want to consider a bike made specifically with bikepacking or dirt road touring in mind. Let's look at those bikes next.

What is a bikepacking bike?

The beauty of bikepacking, with the use of soft luggage strapped directly to the bike, is that virtually any bike can be a bikepacking bike. Mountain bikes, whether rigid or with suspension, offer the stopping power and gearing required to carry camping gear over miles of gravel and dirt roads. But as gravel bikes continue to become more capable off-road machines, the lines have been blurred. The type of bike that suits your bikepacking needs best will depend greatly on where you plan to ride. If you're sticking to pavement and dirt roads, a cyclocross or gravel bike will likely keep you happiest. If you want to ride to a campground at the far end of miles of singletrack, a mountain bike will produce more smiles.

But there are also bikes made expressly for bikepacking. They are extremely versatile machines, robust in nature and built specifically for the needs of the long-haul cyclist. A bikepacking bike will often provide clearance for tires over 2 inches in width, and considerably more in some cases. Frame geometry is on the conservative side, with the goal of imparting low-speed stability. These bikes are often compatible with front suspension and include mounts for carrying gear on the frame and fork. The mounting points can be for racks, additional water bottles, or for cargo cages, which are small supports mounted to a frame or fork that hold stuff sacks full of gear.

Disc brakes handle stopping while low gearing helps on steep hills and rough surfaces. In some cases, they are designed for use with drop bars, at other times, for flat mountain bike bars or sweeping bars like the Jones Loop (see next page).

Bruce Gordon's venerable Rock 'n Road Tour model may have been the first bike made with dirt road touring in mind. Starting in the late '80s, Gordon built his pioneering steel frameset with clearance for 700 × 45mm tires, something extremely rare at the time. Accompanying the bike were stout front and rear racks that he welded from tubular steel. Cantilever brakes, borrowed from mountain bikes, increased stopping power over the caliper brakes then available, and low gears made long stretches of dirt more feasible. That

Gordon's Rock 'n Road Tours also handled beautifully and were made precisely only added to their appeal. Still available in an updated version today, the bike is one of the most admired gravel standards available.

More recently, Salsa's Fargo launched a new generation of bikepackers. Essentially a drop bar 29er with stable off-road geometry and myriad mounting locations for water and gear, the Fargo is now the archetypical bikepacking bike for those exploring double track and gravel roads. Originally rendered in steel, a lighter titanium model was also eventually developed. Although the steel models are still available, Salsa debuted the evolution of the Fargo in the form of the carbon fiber Cutthroat, a Tour Divide racing machine. Still a 29er, the Cutthroat saves weight and uses a clever vibration damping system built into the seatstays to increase long-haul comfort. Other large manufacturers have followed suit, using various materials. All the while, smaller handmade labels, like Bruce Gordon, have carried the custom torch, often producing bikepacking bikes on a bespoke basis.

If you're in the market for a bike that you'll use for both gravel and bikepacking, lean in the direction of a bikepacking rig. It's easy to mount narrower tires on a bike with clearance for 2.4-inch tires, but you can't go the other way. Likewise, it's easier to install taller road gears on a bike with derailleurs capable of low gearing than it is to go the other direction. A bikepacking bike in gravel racing guise may not be quite as agile as a pure gravel machine, but it will absolutely get the job done.

Handlebar selection is made for you when you buy a complete bike, but it is still something worth examining. If the bar on your bike is working for you and you don't have hand, arm, shoulder, or neck issues, then you can skip ahead. If it isn't, know that you're not alone and that there are hundreds of handlebar variations on the market. Whether you ride flat mountain bike–style bars or drop bars, different bends and widths can make a big difference.

If you're on a mountain bike and like the upright position but the handlebar you have isn't for you, consider the Loop bar from Jeff Jones. It offers a series of hand positions for cruising, aggressive riding, and even an aerobar-like forward position. It is also popular in bikepacking circles because the front section of the loop is a good mounting location for lights, GPS units, and other accessories.

Drop bars for bikepacking on less technical terrain, for example the Great Divide, provide more hand positions than most mountain bike bars. This helps avoid hand numbness brought on by long hours in the saddle. Several manufacturers have begun to make off-road drop bars with wider, flared drops and angled top sections. Ritchey's VentureMax bar is the latest to appear, adding to Salsa's Woodchipper, Cowchipper, and Cowbell

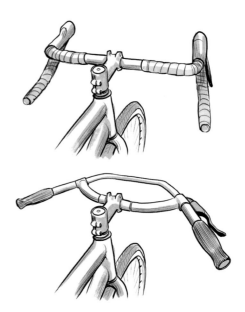

Flared drop bars (top) place your wrists in a natural position. The Jones Loop bar (bottom) is wonderfully versatile.

bars, as well as options from Soma, Alpkit, On-One, and others.

As with gravel, a set of aerobars also has a place on a bikepacking bike if the miles are long or high winds are expected. If the riding is singletrack and technical, there's no need for aerobars. But when battling a stiff headwind for several hours, the increased efficiency and ability to get off your hands makes aerobars worth their weight in gold. They also offer a nice location for accessories, essentially more real estate for GPS units, lights, and map cases.

Route-specific recommendations

It's difficult, and sometimes counter-productive, to make hard-and-fast rules about bikes and their applications. But it becomes more practical to do so when looking at a particular route. When terrain, the amount of climbing, and the surfaces involved are known quantities, recommendations are easier. Past experience gathered from many riders also informs the following suggestions.

The Lauf suspension fork requires no maintenance, but damping is not adjustable.

GREAT DIVIDE MOUNTAIN BIKE ROUTE

For extended travel over the Great Divide Mountain Bike Route (GDMBR), the go-to bike is a 29er mountain bike, perhaps with drop bars for additional hand positions. The large-diameter wheels roll well over obstacles, and replacement tires are easy to find along the way. The excellent braking and wide gear range of a mountain bike are also perfect for weeks of riding with gear.

Simplicity and trailside serviceability reign supreme. With long distances between bike shops, it's important to have a reliable machine, one that you're comfortable maintaining on your own.

Mountain bike drivetrains, with their focus on climbing gears, are the way to go. Whether you decide to use a triple chainring, double chainring, or single chainring is a function of your riding strength and the terrain of your route. For the most challenging sections of the Great Divide, look for the lowest gear you can find. This often means a double or triple chainring drivetrain. If you're sticking to the flatlands, a single-ring 1× drivetrain may be just fine. For extensive riding along the GDMBR, the wider range of a double or triple chainring is most popular for all but the fastest, strongest racers.

Suspension can be a good idea, especially for those looking to tour the route instead of race it. To save weight and eliminate the possibility of problems, many racers eschew suspension and the extra comfort it brings. But suspension forks are

Suspension seatposts, like this Thudbuster, add some comfort to a hardtail frame.

more reliable than ever and getting lighter all the time. They also make the rougher sections much more enjoyable (which is to say one notch above hellacious). Best to have your fork thoroughly serviced before heading out on a long trip like the GDMBR.

If you're looking for a maintenance-free suspension fork, have a gander at the Lauf, a carbon fork designed in Iceland. It employs a series of military-spec fiberglass springs to provide 60 millimeters of progressive suspension. If there is a downside to the fork, it is that you cannot adjust it. There is no damping other than what is provided by the springs. There is also no lockout. The fork is always active.

To enhance comfort without the complexity of a suspension fork or full-suspension bike, some bikepackers use suspension seatposts like Cane Creek's Thudbuster or seatposts designed to afford extra compliance. Syntace, Ritchey, and Ergon all make posts that are designed to flex. Titanium seatposts are also great at absorbing vibration. For the handlebars, extra layers of bar tape or thicker foam grips help mitigate vibration.

In the past, many racers favored mechanical disc brakes for their field serviceability. While still a solid choice, the reliability of hydraulic systems is now well established. Both are worthy of long-distance off-road bikepacking. In either case, ensure that both the rotors and brake pads have plenty of life left in them before setting out. If you've had any inconsistency in your hydraulic brakes, have them bled before leaving. For mechanical disc brakes, make sure that the cables are running smoothly.

OTHER MULTIDAY GRAVEL ROUTE EQUIPMENT RECOMMENDATIONS

Denali Highway. Although the Denali Highway is mostly graded dirt, a bike with 2-inch tires is most at home on this remote road. Be sure to carry enough spares and know how to perform basic repairs, as there are no bike shops along the route.

Trans North California. Like the Great Divide, a 29-inch mountain bike is most at home on the Trans North California route.

With lots of climbing and some singletrack, low gears and wide tires are a wise choice. This route is at times technical and is not for beginners.

Oregon Outback. Again, a mountain bike gets the nod for the Oregon Outback. Gravel bikes with 40mm tires will fly on fast sections but suffer on looser or more technical sections of the route. The toughest sections are in the first half of the route if it's ridden northbound. Water can be scarce, so plan accordingly.

Katy Trail. The Katy Trail, with its groomed gravel path and gentle grades, is a great place for gravel bikes, as well as touring or road bikes with wide, puncture-resistant tires. The Katy Trail has no technical riding, making racks and panniers a good choice for carrying gear.

Great Allegheny Passage and C&O Towpath. Much like the Katy Trail, most of the Great Allegheny Passage and C&O Towpath consist of graded gravel rail-trails. Gentle railroad grades make low gearing slightly less imperative.

Arizona and Colorado Trails. The GDMBR is primarily a gravel route, but both the Arizona and Colorado Trails

A successful Denali Highway setup includes 2-inch tires and plenty of water.

are comprised of significant sections of rugged singletrack. A mountain bike with suspension, whether front only or front and rear, is a more appropriate choice for these routes. Although that suspension could be a liability over 2,768 miles on the Great Divide, it saves the rider from undue abuse on these shorter, more remote tracks. Covering ground at a higher speed also increases the fun quotient.

On the Colorado Trail, many riders have suggested using flat pedals and comfortable hiking shoes. Large sections of the trail are above tree line and include long hike-a-bike climbs. In some cases, especially if ridden in the outer limits of the suggested Colorado Trail season, snow is a very real possibility. Hiking through snow and pushing a bike while wearing slick-soled cycling shoes isn't recommended. Be sure the shoes you choose, whether with recessed mountain bike cleats or not, have a tacky rubber sole. Some experienced veterans recommend a combination of hiking boots and flat pedals to make off-bike time more comfortable.

When covering the entire 750-mile Arizona Trail, bikepackers traverse the Grand Canyon, requiring them to carry their bikes over the 24-mile hike down into the canyon and back up the other side. Paying attention to footwear as well as a reliable, comfortable way to carry your bike on your back is vitally important. Experimenting with backpacks and ways to strap your bike will pay dividends on the trail.

How to carry your load

Traditionally, touring cyclists carried their gear using racks with bags strapped to them, called panniers. This system is still very popular with road cyclists. It's an easy way to carry necessary items in a compartmentalized, organized manner.

The downside of this system for gravel and off-road cyclists is that it significantly slows down the handling of a bike. The bike can be hard to manage at low speeds. In addition, the racks can rattle loose or even break after many miles over bumpy roads. Racks add weight, too, something all cyclists try to avoid.

These shortcomings have led crafty cyclists to develop soft bags that strap directly to their bikes. This approach eliminates the need for racks, and in the case of frame bags, it also centralizes the load, keeping the bike more nimble. Using lightweight fabrics, some strapping, and a bit of Velcro, these bags are capable of truly adventurous bicycle journeys. They also install and remove quickly from whatever bike a rider already has on hand.

Typically, the first bag a fledgling bikepacker should purchase (or make) is a large seat pack. This bag allows a rider to continue to use the water bottle cages

The variety of today's soft bikepacking bags means there's something for every need.

mounted on the frame. A large seat pack complemented by a stuff sack attached to the handlebars usually creates enough capacity for an overnighter. Revelate, Ortlieb, Porcelain Rocket, Apidura, JPaks, Oveja Negra, Nuclear Sunrise, Bedrock Bags, and many, many others produce seat packs of various sizes and designs.

A handlebar-mounted bag should be next on a bikepacker's shopping list. There are essentially two styles. In the first, a harness or sling is designed to carry a dry bag that can be removed from the bike separately. The second option is a bag with integrated mounting. This type can be lighter than the first, but taking it on and off the bike isn't quite as easy. Depending on what you carry and how you like to load your bike, both have advantages. The brands mentioned earlier all produce fantastic examples.

A frame bag is the domain of serious bikepackers. Because it must follow the contours and dimensions of the inside of a bicycle's main triangle, a frame bag is generally a custom item. That said, bike makers Salsa, Surly, Jones, and others offer frame bags that are mass-produced to fit their frames. Partial frame bags, like those made by Revelate and Blackburn, work around the custom issue by producing a series of sizes that are adaptable to many different frames. If you find yourself needing extra space for your bikepacking, a frame bag is a good investment. It will centralize the weight and is a great spot for your heaviest items.

Extra credit gravel trick

Use clear vinyl Gorilla tape to protect the frame and seatpost where your bikepacking bags strap on. The tape prevents scuff marks and blemishes to the paint and is easy to remove later on.

Accessory bags can also be handy when heading out into the wilds. Top tube bags, mounted either behind the stem or in front of the seatpost, add storage for items that a rider wants to keep handy. These bento box–style bags have gained wide popularity in gravel racing as a way to carry food in a quickly accessible spot. Likewise, cylindrical bags mounted on either side of a bicycle's stem are handy spots for an extra water bottle, a camera, or food. Look for options that are reversible, i.e., able to switch from the right side to the left side, so that you can experiment with what works best for you.

Powering your electronics

Many of us use a GPS to record our rides and help with navigation. On multiday trips, a functional GPS can be the difference between a good time and a miserable floundering of a ride. A lighting system can also be handy in case of unforeseen weather or travel delays. Lastly, a way to listen to music and make phone calls is handy. But powering all of them while trying to make miles can be a complicated affair.

Many touring cyclists use electronics that are powered by readily available AA and AAA batteries. This is certainly a nice way to go, as you can easily carry spares and purchase more along the route. Garmin's eTrex GPS series is very popular for exactly this reason. So too are Fenix and Princeton Tec front lights. Many brands produce rear blinking lights so efficient that a single AAA battery will last for months.

If you won't be out long, or if you plan to stay in a hotel from time to time or ride to campgrounds with power outlets, using rechargeable electronics is a possibility. So too are battery packs used to recharge smartphones and GPS units.

For those who regularly go on longer tours, investing in a front dynamo hub, compatible lights, and a USB charging device is a great way to remain off the grid for extended periods. Your forward movement powers the system, and with the use of modern LEDs, the lights on offer are impressive. Schmidt, SP, and Shimano hubs are all high-quality units. Australian

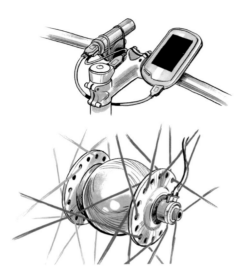

A dynamo hub wire feeds up through the fork steerer to a USB outlet atop the stem.

firm kLite produces systems specifically for bikepacking, with optional switches and USB charging units. Exposure, a British company, makes excellent dynamo headlights that double as battery cells for charging other accessories. Sinewave produces a dynamo-powered USB charging system: Plug in your iPhone and go.

With any of these systems, it's a good idea to test your gear before heading out. Make sure that everything is functioning properly before you rely on a system for your navigation, communication, and lighting. It's never a bad idea to have a backup packed as well, just in case misfortune arises.

Insurance in the wilds

Developing the confidence to tackle the Great Outdoors can be a tricky thing. Preparation goes a long way, but ultimately experience and education take time. Create good habits by carrying water, rain gear, and a fire starter. Even more important, remain aware of your surroundings and act accordingly. Overconfidence can be just as dangerous as a lack of planning.

One way to increase the size of your safety net is through GPS trackers that link to a personalized website to show your position to loved ones at home. DeLorme, a subsidiary of Garmin, and Spot produce rugged, high-quality trackers. Beyond the purchase of the device, a subscription service is also required. In addition to recording your position, trackers feature an SOS button in case of a backcountry emergency; it alerts search and rescue personnel to your situation. Some models also link to your phone, allowing you to send text messages in areas without cell phone reception.

While trackers can add greatly to peace of mind for friends, family, and travelers, it's important to remember that you are still responsible for the costs associated with rescue. A tracker is also no excuse for unnecessary risk-taking. Be safe out there!

Home away from home

There's nothing wrong with staying in hotels, rental cabins, or hostels, but to get to the truly wild places, you need to try

A GPS tracker can link to your own website to keep family informed about your whereabouts.

camping. Sleeping outside and braving the elements is part of the fun of exploring new places. In addition, it can allow you to venture farther afield than if you were relying on permanent structures. What form of shelter you choose will depend on what's already in your closet, your personal comfort zone, a willingness to leave creature comforts at home, and your tolerance for carrying extra weight on your bike.

TENT

When you picture a camping scene, one of the first things you'll envision is a tent. Tents vary in weight, quality, price, and size. There are a lot of factors to balance when purchasing one. For bikepackers who want to minimize bulk and weight, look to

Eric Parsons | Revelate Designs

WORKING TO MAKE GEAR INVISIBLE

Eric Parsons is a longtime adventurer, both on and off a bike. Years ago, as his personal adventures grew in ambition, so too did the need for a reliable way to carry his travel gear in a light, efficient manner. His Revelate bags were born from his experiences during extended trips in India, Patagonia, South America, and Alaska. Now based in Anchorage, Parsons continues to search for ways to make his bags more durable, easier to use, and less obtrusive. Although he was not the first person to produce soft bags for cycling, he was the first to make them widely available. Thanks to this, much credit is due to him for the explosion in bikepacking over the last 10 years.

"All my trips kept planting seeds of what would be ideal."

What is your personal cycling history? And how did you come to make bikepacking bags for a living?
We'll go way back. I got interested in mountain biking while on a family trip in the Canadian Rockies when I was 12. I saw an old mountain bike, a Nishiki. This was in the late 1980s. All of my friends were riding BMX bikes, but I saw that Nishiki and knew that I could go for long rides on it.

I rode mountain bikes throughout high school in New York, playing in mud bogs and breaking things. I kept with it and then started racing in Fort Collins, Colorado, where I went to college. But as I raced, I kept realizing that I was more interested in doing long rides.

Another part of me was really into backpacking and climbing. So I had a bigger-picture idea of mountain adventures.

When the 24 Hours of Adrenalin and 100-mile mountain bike races were blowing up, I did quite a few of those mass-appeal endurance races. I did Montezuma's Revenge, and that became an obsession for two years. Through that race I met a guy doing the Iditasport races in Alaska. He had a bike in his cabin with 50mm Snowcat rims, and a homemade frame bag that his girlfriend or mom had made for him. I had never seen anything like it and thought it was so cool, the whole setup with the big rims and the frame bag. Eventually I got a friend who knew how to sew to make me a frame bag.

Just before that, I started doing some bicycle tours. A good friend asked me along on a big ride. He had heard of a trip in India, so we packed our bags and biked through the Himalayas for a couple months in 2000. That was our shakedown ride. We had no idea what we were doing. We had way too much stuff, pulling it in trailers. After that trip, I realized that if you slimmed everything down, you could do so much more and have a lot more fun.

Eric's designs evolved from personal experience in bikepacking adventures in Patagonia, Alaska, and India, among other places.

Immediately after that trip I wanted to do something totally different, so I booked a trip to Patagonia and all I took with me was the frame bag my friend had made and some stuff sacks strapped to a rear rack. I took the lid off my backpack and strapped it to my handlebars. That ended up being an inspiration for all of Revelate's front pockets. So this tour was the complete opposite of what we had done in India, much lighter and quite a bit more uncomfortable. But that was good. It was a learning experience, especially with regard to gear and packing strategies. That was a turning point.

Shortly after that trip in Patagonia, I moved to Alaska, in 2002. Here I got into winter races, and everyone was using frame bags, usually made by a friend or themselves. One guy out in Palmer was doing small production. A couple years later, I ended up making one of the first versions of the Tangle bag and took that to South America on a six-month trip. That was a hybrid trip with racks and panniers.

All my trips kept planting seeds of what would be ideal. After that trip, I decided that frame bags are where it's at. So I started making frame bags. At one point, I was injured so I decided to see how quickly I could make one. I thought that if I could make one in under four hours, then maybe it was a viable product to make and sell.

I just saw a big void. People were doing these winter races in Alaska and just scratching bags together, home brewing it. I'm a civil engineer by schooling, so I had this engineering mindset, asking, "What could we do better?" I saw it spatially and went to town. Over the course of 2006 to 2007, I would go home every night after work and start cutting fabric and stitching stuff up. That's when I made leaps and bounds.

For a year, all I was doing was supporting the local Alaska fatbike scene, which wasn't even fatbikes yet. It was mostly still Snowcats. Surly had just released the Pugsley, so fatbikes were in their infancy. That scene was growing, and I realized one day that my fledgling business, with a classified ad on the MTBR forum, was keeping me pretty darn busy.

I would come home and sew all night and all weekend just to fill my orders. I was sick of my day job anyway, so I committed myself to it entirely in 2007. I quit my job, bought a real sewing machine, and went for it.

But I felt like there was a big void. It was all or nothing. Racks and panniers were all that was available. You either use those or you make something yourself. But I didn't want to cobble something together. I wanted something that works, and I was sure that other people did too.

That was also right when people like Scott Morris and other key people in the bikepacking movement were doing big trips with funky seat bags that weren't really designed for it, but [they were] still making it happen. I saw a big opportunity and started to work on it.

Bikepacking on Alaska's Iditarod Trail. The challenge, as always, is balancing how much gear you believe you need versus how much you want to carry.

The timing of the growth of bikepacking coincides with the ultralight trips that people like Roman Dial were doing and the improvement in outdoor materials. Have you benefited from that?

Yes. It's easier to find the stuff to pack. You aren't trying to stuff an old-school 2-pound Therm-a-Rest into your pack. Now we have really light Big Agnes tents that weigh 2 pounds. So that definitely helps.

In terms of the material for the bags themselves, that was already there. The climbing community was already using sailcloth and similar materials in technical backpacks. But the bigger picture of the outdoor industry was driven by lightweight backpackers. People were sick of carrying a 60-pound backpack to do an overnighter. That created a momentum for lighter gear.

How did Revelate come about as a company?

It started as Epic Designs in 2007. In 2009, we were forced to change names due to trademark issues. It was a downer, but it was also a good push to legitimize the business, to build a better website, to formalize a lot of aspects of what I was doing.

We're smaller than everybody thinks. Here in Alaska, we're only three people. The reason we're so small is that we don't manufacture everything in Alaska now. Initially I made everything myself in a garage, but then the demand exploded. Around 2010, I was swamped. I needed help. I didn't know manufacturing. I needed some serious backup, and I found it. It's kind of a long story, but that's how some of the production frame bags started. I started with the Tangle bags, and it kept growing from there. With the help, I was able to unload what I was making and free up time. That improved scale considerably and made it possible to sell to dealers.

So we don't currently produce much in Alaska, but that's changing. We're going to start doing high-end limited runs here in Alaska in the coming year.

Any interesting testing mishaps?

It's usually not as glamorous as you think, but with some friends we did some epic beach trips a little while ago. We had

The Revelate ideal: Minimal gear, maximum bliss. The world awaits.

to do quite a bit of bushwhacking. In Alaska, bushwhacking is different because there are all these alders and they grow almost horizontally. It was really thick. We realized we could lay the bikes down on top of the alders and use the bikes' frame bags as a platform to walk across a section. So we lined them all up and took turns crawling from frame bag to frame bag to get through. Then we would bridge the next section of trees. So that was a pretty unexpected, funny use of a frame bag.

Can you suggest any packing tips for bikepackers?

I think the most important thing is to be realistic about how much space you have. If you are short and have limited clearance and a small frame bag, you are going to pack differently than if you have a gigantic bike with tons of room. So gear lists can be helpful, but you have to be realistic about what you're taking in the first place. Next, you need to think about where you're going, the terrain. You should also ask yourself how comfortable you want to be. Or how uncomfortable you're willing to be. The smaller you can get everything, the better.

I would also say that you should get everything inside the bags and have everything as clean as possible. There's a certain glamour associated with having things strapped to the outside. You'll see a spork sticking out the side of the bag or a cup dangling from a seat bag. All that does is get stuff in your way, makes noise, and eventually you're going to lose it.

I see people who have gone with a bikepacking setup but then loaded it like they have a set of panniers. They have stuff strapped all over the place, using the bikes in ways they weren't meant to be used. It's a junk show. They're using Anything Cages with 15-liter stuff sacks nearly exploding with gear. Keep it realistic with how things were designed and how much gear they were meant to carry. Otherwise, it's going to cause problems. There's nothing worse on a trip than having to constantly fuss with your gear. You want it to be invisible.

Lastly, try to keep handlebar weight as light as possible, especially for mountain biking. On the road, it doesn't matter as much. Try to keep water weight low too, whether in the bottom of a frame bag or on the forks.

What does the future of bikepacking bags look like?

In certain regards, I feel like they're good where they are. I think a lot of companies will try to improve on that, but all that's going to happen is adding bells and whistles that you don't really need. Minimalist hardware to get things lighter and more stable is already coming. We'll see some different ways of attaching bags that are quicker and easier.

There are certain things that are driving innovation. For instance, people want to take real trail bikes on rowdy bikepacking trips. And that's great because it's making seat bags that work with full-suspension bikes better.

double-wall backpacking models. These offer good stability in bad weather and typically have great ventilation thanks to mesh on the internal structure protected by a separate outer rain fly.

Even if you plan to go solo, a two-person tent is a smart choice. It will give you extra space for gear without doubling the weight of the tent. It will also let you share the weight if you travel with a partner, though some two-person tents can feel cramped once two people and their gear are inside. Ideally, head to an outdoor store to shop for your tent, taking the time to get inside a floor model to ensure it feels roomy enough. Some favorite makers include NEMO, Big Agnes, Black Diamond, and REI. All of them offer one-, two-, and three- person tents, and larger.

When you want to save weight on a trip where you don't expect many bugs or much bad weather, you can carry only the rain fly, poles, stakes, and a tent-specific footprint, leaving the main tent body at home. This approach, called "fastpacking" or "fast fly," will keep the rain and wind away, but be forewarned it will also allow bugs to enter. Fastpacking requires a tent made for such use. One example is Big Agnes's Copper Spur UL2. MSR and others also produce tents with this possibility built in.

Tents do offer the best protection from wind, rain, and bugs. But that extra coverage comes with some disadvantages. For one thing, a tent is heavier than a simpler setup. And, tent poles can break in strong wind. Also, if you are camping in an area with

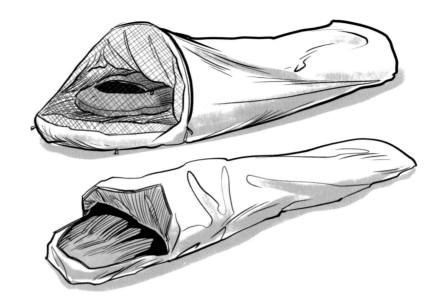

A bivouac shelter (top) offers bug protection. Bivy sacks (bottom) are bare bones.

rocky or very hard ground, driving stakes to secure the tent can be impossible. In that case, you need to get clever, using rocks or trees as anchors. At that point, you may wish you had found an easier setup for the evening, which is where the following alternatives come in.

BIVOUAC SACK

Routinely called a bivy, this is essentially a weather-resistant bag into which you put a sleeping pad and sleeping bag. Some bivy sacks, like Outdoor Research's Helium model, have a pole or two to elevate the surface away from your face

and a waterproof door that can be opened for ventilation; this style of bivy is more formally called a bivouac shelter. Bug netting is available on some bivouac sacks to keep out the creepy crawlies on nights without precipitation. The simplest of bivys, like Montbell's Breeze Dry-Tec Sleeping Bag Cover, may forgo a zipper and use a drawcord to cinch the bag around your face. Some, like those from Survive Outdoors Longer (SOL), are inexpensive and use a heat-reflective material similar to a space blanket. While cheap, they are typically carried as an emergency layer and are somewhat fragile. More robust

Pyramid tents weigh almost nothing. Hammocks get you off the cold, hard ground.

netting. Using a single vertical pole as support, the walls are tensioned using stakes. The shape of this shelter helps it shed rain and snow. It's also a light option with good protection from wind. It can offer good ventilation because it can be pitched with a gap between the bottom of the wall and the ground. NEMO produces a model designed with bikepackers in mind that will provide cover for you and your bike or a couple friends.

TARP

A tarp is a nice way to keep rain off while you sleep. Because it is open sided, it can also provide airflow to keep condensation away. Some users pair a tarp with a bivy for extra warmth. Others use a ground cloth under their sleeping pad and sleeping bag. Whatever you do, you'll want to ensure that you know how to pitch your tarp, orienting it for maximum protection with the wind in mind. Many flat tarps can be pitched in a variety of ways, allowing for different conditions or preferences. Other tarps are shaped for set up in only one configuration.

Tarps save weight over tents because they are essentially only a roof, eliminating the heft of walls and a floor. The drawback is that they aren't as foolproof or weather-proof as a tent. Silnylon and cuben fiber are popular materials, with the former being heavier but less expensive. Mountain Laurel Designs, ZPacks, Sea to Summit, MSR, Big Agnes, and others produce tarps of various shapes and sizes.

bivy sacks use waterproof but breathable materials to keep you dry during a storm. Custom versions are also available from smaller brands, including Borah Gear, Mountain Laurel Designs, Titanium Goat, and MilesGear.

While a bivy may sound ideal at first blush, it can feel claustrophobic and condensation inside the bag can be an issue. Both perspiration and breath exhalations produce moisture that can collect inside a bivy. If the problem is acute, it can dampen your sleeping bag and eliminate its loft and warmth. This makes for an uncomfortable night and requires you to dry your bivy and sleeping bag in the near future. Sleeping with your head outside the bag is helpful, but avoiding condensation is something that requires experimentation.

PYRAMID TENT

In contrast to a double-walled tent with a separate rain fly, a pyramid tent is single walled and does without a floor or bug

Carrying a more capable tent and other gear is easier when two or more riders share the load.

There also exists a hybrid between a tarp and tent. It's made by ZPacks and is called, cleverly, a tarp tent. These are single-wall structures that use a pole or two for support. They often come with bug netting for the side and bottom. This can be a great way to save weight while delivering some protection from rain and bugs.

A true dirtbag option is finding a large piece of Tyvek, a breathable, highly water-resistant building material used to wrap houses before siding is installed, to use as a ground cloth and tarp. Some truly rugged individuals simply wrap themselves in a piece, essentially making a Tyvek burrito, as a very easy-to-fashion shelter.

HAMMOCK

Many campers and backpackers swear by the comfort of a hammock for camping. Hammocks are light, and they also get you away from the cold, heat-sucking ground. But of course you need a place to attach the hammock—not a problem if you're traveling in a wooded area but a conundrum otherwise. If weather threatens, integrated tarps are available. In cold weather, underquilts add insulation. ENO, Hennessy, and Kammok are the principal players in the hammock world.

SLEEPING BAGS

The options available for sleeping bags are staggering. Choice overload is a very real possibility for someone looking to buy a new bag. Unfortunately, much as

with cycling clothing, if you find yourself spending a lot of time camping, you'll likely end up with several sleeping bags so that you can ensure your comfort in varying seasons and weather.

Down or synthetic. Where you live or plan to travel will influence your selection of the insulating material in your bag. Synthetic or down fillers are your options. Synthetic materials are heavier than down but work well even in wet conditions. Down saves weight but can lose its loft when exposed to moisture. Thankfully, with the introduction of hydrophobic coatings, down is now much more resistant to a damp environment. Hybrid insulation is also used in some sleeping bags to ensure warmth in extreme conditions.

With down fillers, there are options regarding different fill weights. Some may argue the merits of the more expensive fill weights, 850 to 900; others contend that fill weight matters little and that saving money on 650 to 750 fill is just fine. Ultimately, that decision is up to you.

Temperature range. The next aspect to consider is the temperature range or rating of the bag. It's important to understand that the manufacturer's temperature rating is only a general recommendation. Each of us has our own sleeping tendencies. Some are comfortable on a chilly 30°F night with only a 50°F rated sleeping bag. Others may

be most comfortable on that same night with a 15°F or 20°F rated bag. It's worth remembering that your sleeping pad has a great deal to do with a night's comfortable rest. So too does a camper's choice of sleeping apparel. Strangely enough, a cozy hat can go a long way toward keeping your toes warm.

If possible, rent your camping gear for your first few bikepacking adventures before you throw down your hard-earned money on a sleeping bag. One uncomfortable night will help inform your decision and give you a better understanding of your particular sleeping needs.

Ground insulation. Many sleeping bags now come with a sleeve along the bottom into which you slip an inflated sleeping pad. This ensures that you don't roll off your pad in the middle of the night. It can also save the weight of insulation on the bottom of the sleeping bag, with a system that relies instead on the loft of the sleeping pad to keep you warm.

QUILTS

Because you compress the insulation upon which you sleep, many argue that carrying a full sleeping bag is a waste of space and weight. A down or synthetic quilt, made using similar materials as sleeping bags, can save weight and increase comfort and versatility. Quilts are also great for campers who feel cramped or claustrophobic in a mummy-style sleeping bag.

Enlightened Equipment, based in Minnesota, produces several quilt models that can be customized for added width or length. Jacks R Better is another popular boutique quilt maker. More recently, NEMO, Therm-a-Rest, and Sea to Summit have begun offering quilt options as well.

A sleeping bag with a bottom sleeve means you won't roll off your pad overnight.

SLEEPING PADS

As mentioned above, the item that insulates you from the ground can have a big impact on how well you sleep. Instead of the temperature ranges used to rate sleeping bags, most pads receive an R-value, a measure of thermal resistance. Without delving too deeply into the arithmetic involved, the higher the rating, the warmer you'll be. The earth is typically much cooler than our body temperature, so having a buffer is a good thing. But more is not always better.

On a hot night, you may want only minimal padding to keep you off the inconsistencies of the ground. In that case, insulation is of little value. Conversely, on a cold winter night, you may need to use a series of pads to isolate yourself from the frigid ground.

To create loft and insulation, sleeping pads are constructed using an inflatable bladder or closed-cell foam (foam that won't soak up water). Inflatable pads can be very light while also compressing a great deal, taking up less room in your bag when not in use. Some are made with a thin layer of synthetic insulation to increase their R-value. When using an inflatable pad, be careful not to place it on sharp objects, as the inflation cells can be somewhat fragile.

Foam pads, on the other hand, don't require kid gloves. They can also be very light and don't require you to huff and puff at the day's end. The downside is that they don't pack down as small as inflatable pads do.

Cooking

Cooking at the campsite can be a great way to save money, steer clear of towns, and go farther afield in your travels. Deciding what to carry, whether it's a backpacking stove, a DIY beer can stove, or some other device, will depend on how long you're traveling, where you plan to go, and what you hope to cook.

In some cases (where allowed), you can rely on a campfire as your range top. Bringing along, or making, a collapsible grill can be useful for roasting veggies and meat. It's also handy to use a grill as a level platform to boil water in a pot atop the coals. Just make sure that you fully extinguish any fires with water so you aren't the accidental or negligent cause of a forest fire. Study up on regulations; it takes much more water than you might think to extinguish a campfire fully.

For quick and efficient cooking, look to backpacking stoves for a light, reliable way to heat water and food quickly. These vary by fuel type: Canister, liquid, tablet, and wood are the four common sources of thermal energy.

Canister stoves use specifically compatible cans of pressurized fuel to deliver a mix of propane and isobutane to the burner. They are very reliable and work well in cold temperatures as long as you take measures to keep the canister, and fuel inside, warm. One way is to keep the canister in your sleeping bag at night. Canister stoves are easy to use, with the ability to control temperature (from simmer to boil), and require less maintenance than a liquid fuel stove. The canisters themselves are sold in different sizes, allowing you to lighten your load for shorter trips or when you have fewer people along. The downside is that the canisters are not reusable or refillable, so they create some waste, and the burners can't use any

Solving the water problem

No matter where we ride, no matter how hot or how cold, how fast or how slow, we need water. How much depends on temperature, altitude, terrain, and individual differences. But a big part of any trip planning should include how you're going to carry and acquire water along the way. If you're sticking to established routes with frequent stops in towns, at rest areas, and at established campgrounds, you may be able to cover your needs without a source of water in the wild. But if you plan to go farther afield, you'll need a way to treat the water you find in lakes, rivers, and streams so it's safe to consume.

Where you travel determines how you treat your water. Do your research to ensure that you cover your bases. Nothing ruins a trip, and sometimes the months afterward, like intestinal issues. The main pests are bacteria, protozoan cysts, and viruses. Read on to better understand the difference between a water filter, generally effective on bacteria and cysts, and a water purifier, capable of eliminating viruses as well.

FILTERING

In the United States and Canada, the biggest concerns are protozoan cysts, like giardia, and bacteria, such as *E. coli* and salmonella. Mechanical water filters will handle these by straining them out. Whether you use an inline filter in your bottle or hydration pack, a pump

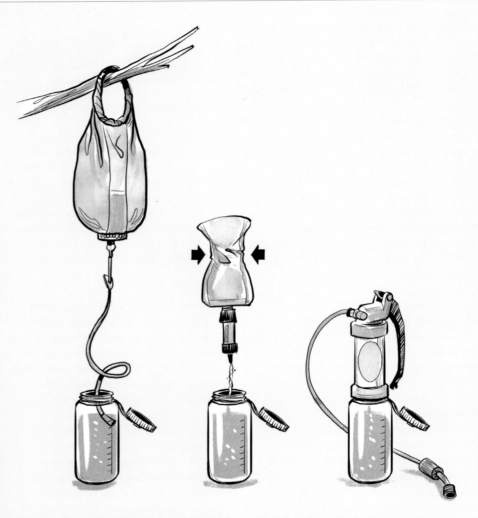

Water filters come in gravity (left), inline (middle), and pump (right) styles. Whichever you choose, be sure to clean the filter regularly as the maker advises.

filter, or a gravity filter, all of them will get the job done. The differences lie in how much time they require, the volume they can handle, and your personal preferences. You may find that one setup is great for a particular route but you prefer another method on a longer journey. Look to companies such as MSR, Sawyer, and Katadyn for options. Also take the time to understand the maintenance required for each filter. Replacement element changes and regular, thorough cleaning of the filter will extend its life and increase its efficiency.

PURIFYING

If you're traveling overseas, particularly in less developed areas, you need to think about viruses as well. Viruses are smaller than bacteria, and some filters can't rid your water of them. Thankfully, there are exceptions. MSR's new Guardian is one example of a pump filter that does eliminate viruses. If you prefer to carry both a filter and a purifier for maximum versatility, there are lots of choices. But bear in mind that you'll want to filter your water before purifying it to maximize your purifier's efficacy. Once filtered, there are several methods for purifying, each with strengths and weaknesses. Depending on your timetable and location, you may change up your method. But if you have questionable water in your future, you'll want to boil it, treat it with iodine, or zap it with UV to kill any viruses floating around.

UV light water purifiers are quick and effective.

Boiling water may sound old school, but it's a highly effective way to make water safe for consumption. The downside is that it requires you stay put and carry fuel for fire. At sea level, you need to boil water for one minute to sterilize it. At altitudes above 5,400 feet, you should increase that to three minutes.

Iodine-based tablets and liquid additives will kill viruses such as hepatitis A and rotavirus, but they require time to activate, up to four hours for very cold water. They also can't handle cryptosporidium and shouldn't be consumed by pregnant women or people with thyroid conditions. MSR, Katadyn,

Potable Aqua, Aquatabs, and Aquamira all produce chemical purifying tabs or drops.

Lastly, you can kill viruses the high-tech way with a UV light purifier. These battery-operated devices are quick and effective, but the water you purify can't be cloudy. So you'll need to pre-filter. An upside is that you never need to buy replacement elements. You will need to carry spare batteries when traveling, though. Both SteriPEN and CamelBak offer UV purifier choices.

WORDS TO DRINK BY

A large caveat to this look at filters and purifiers arises when traveling in areas where the water sources are toxic. Water that is biologically contaminated can generally be treated or filtered as described above, but water sources that are chemically contaminated should be avoided altogether. This can mean agricultural runoff that contains pesticides and mining and industrial runoff that contains chemicals such as arsenic, lead, mercury, and so on. None of the methods I've outlined is capable of removing these dangerous substances.

No matter how you decide to treat your water, you'll want to be sure to keep your hands as clean as possible. Steer clear of areas with livestock whenever possible. Always seek out clear, flowing water. Also, be sure to label your clean and contaminated containers clearly so that you don't accidentally drink from the wrong vessel.

other fuel if you run out of canister fuel. Additionally, it can be tricky to know how much fuel remains in a canister, and fuel costs run a bit higher than with liquid fuel stoves.

Jetboil, MSR, Snow Peak, and Primus are all recognized and highly regarded makers of canister stoves. They vary in price, weight, and performance. Shop around to decide which may be best for you.

Liquid stoves burn fuel that is compressed via a small pump attached to a reusable reservoir bottle. These require priming and a bit of regular maintenance to keep them running at peak efficiency. Where they come into their own is when you're traveling internationally, as many of them, like MSR's WhisperLite International, can burn white gas, kerosene, and unleaded gasoline. They work well on uneven ground and at high altitudes in cold temperatures. And like canister stoves, you can regulate the flame, allowing for simmering.

Monitoring fuel levels is easy to do: just peek into the fuel bottle. While handy, this easy access to the fuel also means that fuel spills are possible. Plus, the total weight of liquid fuel stoves tends to be higher than canisters.

If you're not sure whether you'd prefer a canister or liquid fuel stove, MSR's WhisperLite Universal is made to work with both, lending it great versatility.

Denatured alcohol stoves are another form of liquid fuel stoves, but they burn at a consistent rate and use readily sourced denatured alcohol instead of white gas as fuel. These stoves have no moving parts, typically weigh very little, and burn silently. The flip side is that alcohol burns at a lower temperature than white gas or canister fuel, so cooking can take longer. Trangia, Vargo, Esbit, and others produce alcohol stoves commercially. But if you like to tinker, there are hundreds of beer, soda, or cat food can stove designs available on the Internet. These can weigh only a few ounces and are easy to replace in the event of damage.

Solid fuel stoves, like those from Esbit, are a cinch to use, very inexpensive, and pack down to incredibly small sizes. They use a solid tablet of combustible material that is easy to ignite and use. The tablets burn at a consistent rate, so there is no adjusting the heat, but cooking can take

Camp stoves come in canister, liquid fuel, solid fuel, and wood burning styles.

some time, especially at altitude or in windy conditions. While some bikepackers swear by them, others view them solely as an emergency item.

Collapsible wood stoves are another intriguing option, depending on where you plan to camp. They burn twigs, small branches, and pinecones that you source on the spot. This means that you save carrying the weight of fuel, but if you encounter rain, it can be hard to find dry wood. Likewise, if a fire ban is in effect, using wood stoves is prohibited. Some models are very simple, like Vargo's titanium Hexagon model. BioLite produces a model that both cooks food and boils water while also producing electricity to charge electronic accessories. An integrated battery also powers an adjustable fan that improves the efficiency of the stove and eliminates smoke from the fire inside. The fan settings allow the user to adjust the amount of heat produced by the stove to decrease boil times or lower the heat for simmering.

Some canister stoves have integrated piezo ignitors to light the fire, but in most cases you'll need to carry an ignition source. Both lighters and waterproof matches work well.

When it comes to cookware, look for nesting pots that decrease bulk in your bags. Jetboil, for instance, makes a system that uses the pot to house the stove and fuel canister. Whenever possible, look for dual-use items. There is rarely a need for bowls

Handy to have: nesting pots, rehydrated meals, a pocket knife, and a spork.

unless you're cooking for a crew. Titanium cups and pots can save weight while still conducting heat efficiently. Plastic works well for cups or bowls that won't serve as cooking vessels.

When it comes to utensils, the spork, a combination fork and spoon, is still popular. The concept is produced in plastic, steel, aluminum, and titanium. If you plan on eating dehydrated food

reconstituted with hot water, carrying an extra-long spoon makes scraping the bottom of the foil bag a lot easier. The bag also simplifies clean up. Simply boil water in your pot, pour it into the foil bag, and eat directly from the bag. Then pack the bag out the next day.

A folding knife or pocketknife is also extremely useful when camping and bikepacking. Some consider them an

A fast-running stream can be a good source for fresh water, but be sure to check for animal tracks before pitching your tent.

essential item, along with a fire starter kit, whenever venturing into the wilderness. Whatever you carry, be sure to maintain the blade, keeping it sharp. A dull blade is a liability, leading to more injuries than a sharp edge.

Hygiene

As in any kitchen, the work is not done when meal is over. To keep your bike bags clean and avoid illness, it's important to wash your dishes and hands before and after eating. Carry a small bottle of eco-friendly biodegradable soap to keep things tidy. Be sure to use clean or purified water when washing up; but if you rinse with contaminated water, it's a wasted effort.

Personal hygiene is also an imperative. Crush your toilet paper flat and carry it in a plastic Ziploc or dry bag to ensure rain does not get to it. A small travel pack of wet wipes can also be nice for cleaning up after a long day on the trail.

When it comes to your relieving yourself, be sure to use facilities when possible. If you're not in a campground with restrooms, be sure to carry out any trash. As for bowel movements, there are two options: bury solid waste in a hole 6 to 8 inches deep and at least 200 feet from water, campsites, and the trail, or carry it out. Yep, you read that right. In some high-use areas, trail users are required to pack out everything, including their own solid waste. Be sure to read up on regulations before you head out.

For cleaning yourself between showers, it's a good idea to carry a small bottle of Dr. Bronner's. It can be used as shampoo, body wash, toothpaste (use only a drop or two), and a laundry detergent. Err on the side of using less, as it is sold undiluted.

Multiday adventure packing checklist

To build upon the daily ride checklist found at the end of Chapter 6, here is a suggested list of items that you should consider at minimum when heading out for a longer adventure. Again, if you don't know how to use something, take the time to educate yourself or seek help. Having it along is of little use unless you're confident in its function.

FOR LONG RIDES

- Water treatment method
- Maps, GPS, compass
- Electronic insurance in the form of a Spot Tracker or DeLorme
- First-aid kit
- Shelter: Tent, tarp, bivy, planned hotel/cabin/hut/yurt
- Food and water and resupply plan

Bicycle repair kit
See the daily ride checklist and add the following:
- Spare clipless pedal cleat
- Safety pins
- Needle and thread
- Brake pads
- Length of chain and extra quick links
- Assortment of spare bolts
- Brush for cleaning drivetrain
- Spare batteries for lights and GPS
- Leatherman tool or similar with pliers and knife
- Emergency fire-making kit (waterproof matches, waxed kindling, lighter)
- Single-use Super Glue
- Tenacious tape for tent, clothing, sleeping bag repair

Vlad Dolinksy, originally from Ukraine, now builds his Vlad Cycles in New Jersey. Combining custom racks and Andrew the Maker bags, the Dirt Tourer carries camping essentials in style.

⑧ BUILDING YOUR GRAVEL DREAM MACHINE

For adventure cyclists who ride on gravel and remote, forgotten tracks, there has never been a better time to build a custom bike. Whether you commission a custom handmade frame from a local builder or purchase a stock frameset and assemble it into a complete bicycle, the process ensures that your new bike meets your technical and aesthetic preferences.

Certainly the most cost-effective way to purchase a new bicycle is to buy a complete one from a local bike shop or direct-to-consumer producer. The buying power of large bicycle manufacturers makes the economics such that you could never assemble one for less. So from a value perspective, look first at stock complete bikes.

For many gravel riders and bikepackers, showroom stock is a great way to get rolling on a new bike. With perhaps a few changes to accommodate your fit (think saddle, seatpost, handlebars, and stem), most riders will find themselves aboard a machine that is more than capable of delivering exceptional experiences that can last a lifetime. While it's a cliché, it really isn't about the bike. Getting outside, exploring new places, meeting new people, and testing personal limits are what draws so many to gravel riding. The bike is simply a conduit.

Where stock bicycles fall short is when a rider has particular biomechanical needs, wants to try a specific geometry, feels the imperative for personal expression through a singular aesthetic, or desires to hand-select individual components. In the last case, it's worth considering the purchase of stock frame and fork and building the bike from there. This can save money and still accomplish your goals. Likewise, having a stock bicycle custom-painted is an easy way to personalize a bike without the expense of a custom-made frame.

If, on the other hand, it's the dimensions of the frame that are in question and no stock options exist, you'll need to go custom. Of course, there are other obvious reasons to consider custom. Perhaps you've fallen in love with the look of a particular builder's frames. Construction is yet another reason. If a fillet-brazed steel frame is your idea of a perfect bike, your only option is custom. The mainstream cycling industry works almost exclusively in TIG-welded frames and molded or lugged carbon fiber.

The place of origin of handmade custom frames is also a draw for many cyclists. Perhaps you'd like a made-in-Colorado titanium frame. In that case, Moots, Mosaic, and Black Sheep can fill that desire with spectacular results. How about a lugged steel frame from Baltimore? Chris Bishop can help. Interested in a bike built by one of the founding fathers of mountain biking? Call Steve Potts in Petaluma.

Bespoke built

If you've decided that it's time for a custom bike, there are two key first steps you must take before you head down the bespoke path. The first is defining how you'll use the bike. Do you need custom geometry to better accommodate your biomechanical needs? Are you hoping for a quiver killer, one bike for all things? Is this purely a gravel race bike, built solely for competition? Will you load up the bike and head out for weeks at a time? Will the bike pull duty as a commuter? This determination, more than any other, should inform what type of bicycle you build.

Second, you must establish a budget. Ideally, you will do this after a bit of research to make sure your figure is realistic. Thankfully, there are many gravel and bikepacking bikes that have been assembled from modest means. In those cases, expect a steel or aluminum frame. Of course, bikes on the other end of the spectrum, custom exotica, are also readily available. Here you'll find titanium and even custom carbon fiber frames. In any case, note that complex paint jobs can add significantly to the final price tag. Also, explore whether you plan to buy a complete bike, fully assembled, from the builder or if you will purchase the frame separately from the components.

While you never want to waste a builder's time, be sure to discuss what you have in mind before putting down a deposit. You want to make sure that communication is easy, with both parties making themselves clear about pricing, the build timeline, and whether the builder can meet your requests.

Advocate Cycles Hayduke 27.5+ packed for Colorado Trail

- Eric Hockman's 27.5+ steel Hayduke has 3-inch wide tires for traction on trails. It can also be run with 29er wheels and tires.

- Front suspension takes the edge off of the rougher sections of the Colorado Trail, the route for which the bike was assembled.

- Hockman uses a 1× drivetrain with a wide-ratio rear cassette on his Hayduke. The simplicity is great for backcountry expeditions.

- Joe Tonsager of JPaks, a custom bikepacking bag maker in Denver, sponsors Hockman and crafted his bags. The frame pack is made specifically for the Hayduke, with a matching top tube bag.

- Before his Colorado Trail trip, Hockman carefully experimented with different ways of loading the bike to maintain good handling and keep weather-dependent items close at hand. Because he rode with his girlfriend, they were able to share items and cut total packed weight.

- Advocate Cycles donates its profits to several nonprofit advocacy groups including People for Bikes, Adventure Cycling Association, and IMBA.

When it comes to the design process, each builder is a bit different. Some work directly with customers, while others go through a dealer network. In either case, you want to be sure that your fit concerns are addressed. This usually entails an extensive measurement process, often beginning with a bike you currently own and then moving on to an adjustable fitting bike to evaluate changes. Be sure to bring up any recurring issues you've had, such as tendinitis, numb hands, or a sore neck.

Part and parcel of the fit is handlebar choice. Be sure that you have decided upon the general type of bar you'd like to use, as it will affect your fit and the geometry of the frame. Top tubes are longer for flat mountain bike bars and Jones Loop bars compared to frames designed for drop bars. This means that changing bar type later can be difficult.

In an ideal world, both the fitter/bike shop and the frame builder you settle upon will have experience in gravel riding and bikepacking, depending on the intended purpose of your new bike. In some cases, the builder is the fitter. Discuss both what you've liked and disliked about your past bikes when you meet. Did you love the way your gravel bike handled but you felt too stretched out? Maybe you're looking for more stability and confidence in high-speed loose gravel. Did your bikepacking bike handle like a dream when unladen but transformed into a wet noodle once your camping gear was strapped on? All of these

problems have solutions. The possibilities are endless, and a veteran frame builder will be able to translate your preferences into frame dimensions and construction.

Once the geometry is settled, determined by your biomechanical needs and the intended purpose of the bike, it's time to discuss individual, fascinating details. Do you plan to use fenders? What about rack mounts? Or perhaps you'd prefer to have the rack permanently brazed to the frame to avoid rattle-prone fasteners. Some frame builders are now coordinating with frame bag manufacturers and fitting threaded inserts to the inside of the main triangle to which the bags are bolted. This keeps the bag secure without the use of Velcro straps. The look is very clean, and this setup eliminates scuffing from the bag and its straps as they move around on rough roads.

If you have a long-distance gravel or bikepacking bike in mind, you may want to consider a dynamo hub. If the idea of running front and rear lights powered by that hub has you excited, be sure to mention it. The frame builder can provide internal routing for the necessary wiring.

There are constant opportunities for innovation. Nicholas Carman, world traveler and creator of the Gypsy by Trade blog, wanted a better way to portage his bikepacking bike when the trail became too steep to ride or when he encountered fallen trees. Working with Whit Johnson of Meriwether Cycles, a crossbar was added

Chumba Stella 29er
packed for a bikepacking tour

- Chumba's Stella is a titanium hardtail with sliding rear dropouts, which are great for adjusting the wheelbase or to set up the bike as a single speed.

- Neil Beltchenko raced this bike in the 2015 Tour Divide to an incredible third-place finish.

- For the race, Beltchenko carried even less than is pictured and swapped the Fox suspension fork for a rigid unit.

- Camo Wanderlust bags adorn the Chumba. When purchasing a Stella, Chumba offers a package that includes a suite of bags and a dynamo front hub.

- The seat bag is Porcelain Rocket's Mr. Fusion model, a harness-type bag with a separate dry bag that includes a support/brace that clamps to the seatpost and eliminates bag sway.

- Beltchenko carries a bottle underneath the down tube as a way to keep the center of gravity lower while increasing capacity.

Nicholas Carman asked Meriwether Cycles to add a portage handle to his frame.

to connect the top tube and driveside seatstay. This bar acts as a convenient handle when lifting the bike and doesn't add significant weight.

What bottom bracket standard would you like to use? If you don't have a strong opinion, ask the builder for advice (though I'll advocate for a threaded bottom bracket in almost every situation). Part of the beauty of a custom frame is that you get to learn something new in the process of buying it. Bottom bracket standards don't interest you? Defer to the builder. Your level of involvement is up to you.

When speaking with your builder, you need to have a solid idea of the parts you plan to install on the bike. This decision informs the dimensions of the frame just as much as

your fit, especially with regard to chainstay length and chainring and tire clearance.

Components befitting your frame

After the fit of the frame, tire size and gearing should be your primary focus. How wide and how low do you need to go? Be honest with yourself, especially with respect to gearing, and err on the conservative side. Bringing ego into these decisions isn't useful. As mentioned earlier, a bicycle appropriate for bikepacking will also work for gravel racing. You can always install narrower tires and taller gears on a bikepacking ride if need be. But the opposite is not true. You can't fit 2-inch tires into a typical gravel

Specialized Diverge
packed for dirt road touring

- The Diverge models from Specialized are road bikes with added tire clearance, making them great for exploration. Shown is the mid-range, aluminum frame, carbon fork Comp DSW XI version.

- The Diverge aluminum frames also provide rear rack mounts if you prefer to use a trunk or panniers. The fork is compatible with a lowrider front rack. Luggage options abound on the Diverge.

- Specialized's Burra Burra partial frame bag carries plenty while still providing access to water bottles on the frame. Porcelain Rocket makes the now-weathered rear bag and front harness. Accessory bags on the top tube and beside the stem keep items like food, wallet and camera handy.

- SRAM I× gets the nod for drivetrain, but the front chainring is quite a bit larger than on mountain bikes, a 46-tooth in this case. The cassette is SRAM's 10–42 range. This gearing is great for use as a gravel bike but limited for a touring bike. Keep your load light on such a bike. Also consider a smaller chainring and wider-range cassette.

- The frame makes plenty of room for 700×35 tires, and reportedly 38mm tires can be shoehorned in. Be sure to consider the possibility of mud in your travels, though, and go narrower if you expect it.

A belt drive mated to an internal-gear hub minimizes maintenance and noise.

bike (without a wheel size change). Nor can a derailleur designed for a maximum cassette size of 28 teeth accommodate a 40-tooth cassette. On the other hand, if you don't plan to bikepack in mountainous areas, then a gravel bike with clearances for 40mm tires will likely save weight over a bikepacking machine.

GEARING

The second decade of the 21st century has brought new levels of technological advancements to the cycling world. Many of them, thankfully, are made with adventure in mind and not just for emaciated professionals toiling away on the paved mountain roads of Europe. As you imagine your new dream bike, it's likely that you already have a preference regarding drivetrain brand. If so, roll with it. One of the most important things a cyclist can carry into the wilderness is confidence in his or her steed.

Here is a brief overview of the state of the drivetrain union, beginning with our bold new age of electricity. If you find yourself with the world as your oyster, then you can likely afford to consider electronic

Santa Cruz Chameleon 27.5+
packed for New Mexico Offroad Runner

- Built to tackle nearly 500 miles of New Mexico dirt roads, this Santa Cruz has features to handle rough roads in an arid climate. The aluminum frame is the affordable Chameleon model, with a threaded bottom bracket and a stock bottle mount on the underside of the down tube.

- The drivetrain is a 1× setup from SRAM. Race Face supplies the bars, stem, seatpost, crank and wide AR 40 rims that support Maxxis Rekon + 2.8-inch tires. Brakes have been swapped from stock for a set of Shimano hydraulic stoppers.

- Luggage is a mixed bag, with Bedrock, Porcelain Rocket and Oveja Negro all used in various spots. The frame and seat bag are from Porcelain Rocket and use some cuben fiber material to save weight, a custom feature. A spare tube is taped to the strut of the Mr. Fusion brace.

- Water, water everywhere. To carry a larger than normal bottle, a Topeak Modula cage is fitted to the underside of the down tube. A pair of inexpensive cages are hose-clamped to the fork legs. Bottles are then strapped for security over bumpy terrain.

The Pinion gearbox centralizes its machinery mass at the bottom bracket.

Salsa Redpoint 27.5
packed for southwest bikepacking

- Salsa's Redpoint mountain bike is made for the rowdy stuff. With 150mm of travel and 27.5-inch wheels, it's a singletrack slayer.

- Kurt Refsnider has this bike loaded for a 3-day trip around the Navajo Mountain in an area of the Navajo Nation along the Utah/Arizona border.

- Making use of a dropper post makes riding technical terrain easier but it does limit the amount of gear that can be carried behind the saddle. Refsnider is using a prototype Revelate Designs bag on his seatpost.

- While expensive, there is no reason to shy away from carbon fiber. Both the frame and cranks are carbon. Many bikepackers have had great experiences with carbon rims as well.

- A sharp eye will notice spare spokes taped to the seatstay of Refsnider's bike.

- Tape on the fork leg is there for times when Refsnider installs a bottle cage. It protects the finish of the fork and aids in keeping the cage from slipping.

shifting. Shimano Di2, SRAM eTap, and Campagnolo EPS are all offered in packages that are gravel appropriate. They provide road gearing that, with the use of a compact crank, is sufficient for gravel cyclists. As with many things in life, each manufacturer has its strengths and weaknesses. If your interest is piqued by the lure of electrons, then do your research to find the group that suits you best. All of the current electronic groups offer extremely accurate shifting that won't degrade in bad conditions because there are no shift cables that can become contaminated. They also reduce the amount of effort required by riders to perform a shift. Over long distances, this is a distinct advantage (Race Across America participants were early adopters of electronic shifting for this reason in particular).

If you're looking for electronic shifting more appropriate for bikepacking, Shimano's XTR and XT Di2 mountain bike groups bring digital shifting to the world of mud and dust. Both of them can be shifted using either flat bar or drop bar Di2 shifters, so Frankenbike creations are as easy as plugging in a few wires.

Of course, all this wizardry comes at a cost. Electronic drivetrains are very

expensive, and because of that, you're less likely to find replacement parts in stock in rural bike shops. This is something to consider if you're heading out for the hinterlands.

There is also the issue of battery charge. All of the current systems have plenty of capacity for weeks of heavy use. But if you are attacking the Great Divide, heading across Australia, or undertaking some similar extended epic, you need to calculate whether you'll need to recharge along the way—and if so, where and how you'll do it.

Mechanical shifting is how most of the world changes gears, and that's not a bad thing: Cable-actuated shifting has made great leaps forward in recent years. Very popular for mountain biking is the previously mentioned 1× drivetrain, using a single front chainring and a wide-ratio rear cassette. SRAM currently leads the 1× range game with its Eagle mountain bike group. The group uses a single front ring and a 12-speed rear cassette with a 10- to 50-tooth spread to give you wings.

Not far behind is Shimano with its 11–46 cassette paired with a 1× crank. Some adventurers have experimented with using Shimano's widest cassette with a double chainring setup. While Shimano does not encourage this arrangement, riders have found that it will work if a long cage derailleur is used and careful attention is paid to chain length.

The two significant upsides to 1× drivetrains are weight savings and simplified shift patterns. The rider has only to concentrate on harder or easier, getting there by shifting one lever. It does keep things simple. While 1× systems are great for gravel riding, I hesitate to recommend them for bikepacking, where the additional weight of camping gear means that an exceptionally low gear is often required. Simultaneously, that extra weight means that descents, particularly on the road, can be very swift. Depending on the front chainring installed, it's easy to quickly run out of gears with a 1× system.

For most bikepackers except the very fittest, a double chainring drivetrain is still the way to go if you're hoping to ensure an adequately low climbing gear while maintaining a reasonable gear for road cruising. A double setup provides more versatility too if the bike you're assembling will be used for a variety of bikepacking, gravel, and perhaps commuting duties.

Although some have proclaimed that the front derailleur is dead, the triple is alive and well in bikepacking and bicycle touring circles. Triple chainring drivetrains, those with three front gears, provide an exceptionally wide gear range while maintaining small rear cassette steps. With so many gears available, the perfect ratio for almost any situation is available. Conscientious cyclists aboard triples can also maintain better chainline, keeping the chain as straight as possible between front and rear gears. This helps to prolong drivetrain life. Shimano's latest 11-speed

Mosaic Cycles GT-1
for daily gravel riding

- Using double-butted titanium tubing and custom-shaped stays, Mosaic's GT-1 is considered the ultimate custom gravel bike by many. This bike, owned by Mosaic's founder Aaron Barcheck, won Best Gravel Bike at the 2017 North American Handmade Bicycle Show.

- The fork is Enve's Gravel Road (GRD) model with a 12mm thru axle, Flat Mount braking posts, and an integrated clip-on fender. It has room for 38mm tires without the fender or 35mm with the fender installed.

- The precise custom paint from Spectrum Paint Powder Works coats the frame, Enve fork, stem, handlebar, and seatpost, both fenders, and the Silca frame pump. Notice that the rear section of the non-corrosive titanium frame is left bare to keep grease away from the paint.

- Continuing the Enve theme is a pair of M50 tubeless carbon fiber wheels.

- A Shimano Dura-Ace Di2 electronic drivetrain is shifted with Shimano R785 hydraulic brake levers.

- Clement Strada USH 32mm tubeless tires are a fast file tread tire perfect for a mix of tarmac and dirt roads.

mountain bike groups are offered with a triple option, but finding parts in North America is a bit difficult. On the other hand, 10-speed triple parts are still easily sourced; so too are 3×9 parts. If you're buying new, though, stick to the latest generation.

Also noteworthy are the engineering wonders made by Rohloff and Pinion, German firms known for producing very reliable components. The Rohloff is a 14-speed internally geared rear hub. Its mechanism is entirely hidden inside the rear hub shell, keeping all essential parts far from harm's way. Long-distance touring and racing cyclists have experienced virtually maintenance-free performance from Rohloff's Speedhub, and it continues to be a popular choice for globe circumnavigators because only periodic oil changes are required. The Rohloff requires the use of a twist-style shifter compatible with mountain bike bars, although aftermarket road shifters are also available. Frames must likewise be compatible with the Rohloff hub, which requires a special rear dropout. If the Rohloff system interests you, be sure to mention it to your frame builder.

The Pinion is a gearbox system with several options from 6 to 18 gears. Using automotive-style spur gears, the Pinion places its mechanism at the bottom bracket, lowering and centralizing its weight. It too uses a twist shifter, with options for road and mountain bike bars.

Both the Pinion and Rohloff systems can be paired with a Gates Carbon Drive belt in lieu of a chain. Lighter than a chain and requiring less maintenance, a belt drive is a great choice for long-distance and adventure cyclists. Carrying a spare belt is recommended, however, as sourcing one in the wilds of Wyoming or elsewhere will take some doing.

MIX AND MATCH: MOUNTAIN GEARING AND DROP BARS

If you like the appeal of mountain bike gearing but are a staunch drop bar rider, have no fear. There are several solutions to the mix and match question, from single-ring (1×) to triple-ring drivetrains. Establish the range you'd like to accomplish and then read on.

First up is the simplest. If you're a fan of 1× drivetrains, then SRAM is an easy choice for drop bar users. The firm's Force1 rear derailleur, in its long cage form, and drop bar road shifter are compatible with the same 10–42 cassette used on the company's mountain bike groups. Note that you need an XD Driver–compatible rear hub to use this ratio.

To do the same with Shimano, you'll need to employ aftermarket components to pair 11-speed road shifters with 11-speed mountain bike derailleurs. A small company called Wolf Tooth produces the Tanpan, a cable pull ratio converter that allows the use of Shimano 11-speed drop bar shifters with Shimano 11-speed mountain bike rear derailleurs. This opens up great possibilities for low gearing using readily available parts. It also makes 2×11 mountain gearing a possibility with drop bars.

Gevenalle shifters gracefully adapt mountain bike gearing to drop bars.

The Tanpan converter lets you use Shimano road bike levers with mountain derailleurs.

Another way to accomplish double or even triple mountain bike gearing on a drop bar bike is by using a set of brake/shift levers from Gevenalle, a small company in Portland, Oregon. Its levers are made to shift mountain bike derailleurs, and they do so extremely well. They are also easy to install and simple to maintain trailside, as there are no hidden parts tucked inside the brake lever. If there is a downside, it's that a rider using Gevenalle shifters can only perform a gear change from the hoods. That's a small price to pay for lightweight, affordable mountain gearing on a drop bar bike.

Lastly, the use of bar-end shifters will also make single, double, or triple mountain bike gearing possible on a drop bar bike. Many long-distance riders love the rugged simplicity of bar-end shifters, despite their location at the end of the drops.

BRAKES

As discussed in Chapter 6, the brakes on a bike are just as important as the drivetrain. Disc brakes reign supreme in the gravel and adventure world. Rim brakes certainly still have a place in the hearts of those who crave simplicity, but if you're building your dream bike, why not take advantage of advances in braking technology?

Because of the loose nature of gravel roads, brake modulation and feel are vitally important. Too much power will have you skidding, and too little power will leave you careening. Neither is a good situation. The smallest rotor size typically recommended by manufacturers is 160mm. Larger riders may want to consider a larger front rotor. Just be sure that your bike's fork is compatible before purchasing a larger rotor and the matching caliper adapter.

While modulation is still important for bikepackers carrying the added weight of camping gear, spare clothing, extra food, and water, absolute power is a bit more important. The use of larger disc brake rotors is worth consideration. A 180 or even a 200mm front rotor paired with a 180 or 160mm rear rotor is a great bikepacking combination, especially on full-suspension bikes.

Exotic brake options are available, but sticking with popular brands is a wise way to go. It makes servicing and finding spare brake pads, whether you decide on hydraulic or mechanical brakes, a much easier affair, whether you race gravel or traverse mountain ranges. (For a more in-depth look at the pros and cons of disc brakes, see Chapter 6.)

Whatever you decide, pay close attention to the condition of your brakes. Check for pad and rotor wear. If you see any hydraulic fluid leaking, do *not* go for a ride. Seek help at your local bike shop. With mechanical disc brakes, be sure that the brake cables are running smoothly. Taking a few moments to check your bike before each ride is worth every second.

Epilogue

In the first pages of this book, I tried to paint a beautiful picture of gravel riding and racing through the lens of my first experience at the Dirty Kanza 200. Now that you've read this far and the hook has been set for your own gravel adventure, I suppose it's safe to fess up about the rest of that day.

While the day began in a bucolic fashion, Mother Nature decided that the going was too easy. A violent storm made its way over the course while I was somewhere around 70 miles from the finish. Sideways rain and strong winds blew me off the road. After hunkering down in a ditch for a few minutes, I decided that the worst of the weather had passed. I was offered a ride from a passing truck, but seeing a rider approaching, I decided to carry on. I rode with this racer, a fellow from Iowa named Mike Johnson, for several miles until a turn onto an MMR, or minimum maintenance road—a dirt double track that farmers use to access their fields. After the rain, the road was a nearly impassable gully of muck. Riders ahead were carrying their mud-clogged bikes. None were riding. I slogged through, eventually crossing a fast-running creek that I used to de-mud my wheels and drivetrain. Thankfully, an aid station wasn't far away.

There, LeLan Dains, my crew that day and now a co-owner of Dirty Kanza, handed me a Coke and ran off with my bike to wash it. I thought for sure that the race would be cancelled. My morale was low. I still had 45 miles to go, and daylight was fading. But the weather had turned again, this time for the better. At the urging of LeLan, for whom my continuing was never a question, I rode on into a gorgeous Kansas evening. Hours later, after starting at 6 a.m., I crossed the line at 10:57 p.m., dazed, thirsty, hungry, aching, and deliriously happy.

Amazingly, there was a cheering crowd at the finish line, a group that included Jim Cummins, the Kanza promoter. After my ordeal, I was treated like a hero. Someone took my bike. Another helped me hobble to a chair. While I felt completely empty, my heart was full, welling up with the emotion of pushing myself so profoundly. The day had started postcard perfect, but the way it wrapped up was even better. When I had toed the line that morning, I wasn't sure that I could finish such a long race. When the conditions conspired against me, I almost hoped for a reprieve. But thanks to the examples around me, I learned to endure, a lesson that has served me well in subsequent years in all my endeavors, both on and off the bike.

I encourage you to go out there and challenge yourself. You'll discover that you are capable of much more than you ever imagined.

Resources

Adventure Cycling Association
www.adventurecycling.org

Arizona Trail Association
www.aztrail.org

Bikepacker.com
www.bikepacker.com

Bikepacking.com
www.bikepacking.com

Chesapeake & Ohio Canal Towpath
www.nps.gov/choh/planyourvisit/
hikingandbiking.htm

Colorado Trail
www.coloradotrail.org

Denali Highway
www.alaska.org/guide/
denali-highway

Great Allegheny Passage
www.gaptrail.org

Katy Trail
www.bikekatytrail.com

Leave No Trace
www.lnt.org

Oregon Bikepacking
www.oregonbikepacking.com

Riding Gravel
www.ridinggravel.com

Trans North California
www.transnorthcalifornia.blogspot.com

Index

Acknowledgments

Thank you to the many kind people in my life who inspire my love of cycling. Your camaraderie, advice, and generosity of spirit and resources made creating this book an absolute pleasure. In particular, I would like to express gratitude to the Barchecks, Neil Beltchenko, Adam Bergman, Jason Boucher, Jordi Cantal, Miguel Crawford, Jim Cummins, LeLan Dains, Ali Deane, Paul Errington, Elisha Everhart, Jason Gaikowski, Stephan Geiss, Greg Gleason, Corey Godfrey, Yuri Hauswald, Eric Hockman, Mike Johnson, Ted King, Sam Maffett, Nathan Mawkes, Michael "Mac" McCoy, the McKenney family, Joe Meiser, Meredith Miller, Tim and Kristi Mohn, Austin Morris, Ross Muir, Eric Parsons, JD Pauls (RIP), Jay Petervary, Rick Plite, Marlene Ragot, Kurt Refsnider, Sylvain Renouf, the Reynolds family, Mike Riemer, Matt Roy, Rebecca Rusch, Neil Shirley, Chris Skogen, John Stamstad, Mark "Guitar Ted" Stevenson, Joe Stiller, Tara Stone, Burke Swindlehurst, Joe Tonsager, Sandy Whittlesey, Barry Wicks, Lael Wilcox, Bobby Wintle, Mackenzie Woodring, and Tyler Wren.

Thanks also to Charles Chamberlin for his maps and design, Charlie Layton for his illustrations, Vicki Hopewell for art direction and photo research, and Ted Costantino for concept and editing.

About the Author

Born in Indiana, Nicholas Legan found cycling at an early age through the Boy Scouts and was racing by the age of 13, his parents lovingly shuttling him to races around the Midwest. Legan studied French and journalism at Indiana University and spent his junior year in the south of France. After a move to Colorado, he grabbed an opportunity to work as a mechanic for professional road racing teams. He traveled the world for the next seven years, working all three Grand Tours, the world cycling championships, and the 2008 Olympics. He then traded his wrenches for a laptop and began a career as a cycling journalist. He served as the technical editor for *VeloNews* and currently holds the same position with *Adventure Cyclist* while also freelancing for several additional cycling publications. Nick lives with his wife, Kristen, and their dog, Coriander, in Longmont, Colorado, a gateway to exceptional gravel.

Credits

ART DIRECTION
Vicki Hopewell

FRONT COVER DESIGN
Kevin Roberson

INTERIOR DESIGN, MAPS, AND COURSE PROFILES
Charles Chamberlin

ILLUSTRATIONS
Charlie Layton

PHOTOGRAPHS

241Photography, pp. 10, 14, 29, 30, 31, 32, 33, 111 (right)
3T Cycling, p. 216
Darren Alff, pp. 178 (left), 179 (top, bottom right), 180 (right), 181 (top)
Apidura, p. ix
ASO, p. 137 (right)
ASO/Htarieux, p. 136 (top)
ASO/MMolle, p. 135
ASO/AVialatte, pp. 136 (bottom), 137 (left)
Ben Barnhart, pp. 8, 13, 73, 74, 75, 76
BarYak, p. 18
Marcel Batlle, p. 117 (right)
Neil Beltchenko, p. 263

Ramsey Bentley, p. 205
Charles Bingham, p. 149
John Blackwell, pp. 23, 25 (bottom right), 26
Laurent Brossard, pp. 101, 103, 104, 105 (left)
Caminade, p. 105 (right)
Ewan Campbell, p. 108 (top right)
Cane Creek Cycling Components, p. 238 (right)
Nicholas Carman, pp. 153, 154, 200, 204, 206, 234, 239, 264
Patrick Carrigan, p. 71 (right)
Dave Chiu, p. 77
Eddie Clark, pp. 143, 144, 145, 146, 147
Aaron Colussi, p. 15
Conservation Foundation of Missouri Charitable Trust, p. 181 (bottom)
Mike Curiak, p. 152
Don Daly, p. 71 (left)
Catherine Fegan-Kim, pp. vi, xiv, 59, 60 (bottom), 61 (bottom right), 62, 63, 64
Doug Frederick, pp. 166, 167 (bottom right), 168 (left, top right), 169
Gevenalle, p. 272
Giant Bicycles, p. 214
Cass Gilbert, pp. 265, 267
GU Energy, p. 16

Linda Guerrette, pp. 3, 17, 27 (middle, right), 53, 54, 55, 56, 79, 80, 81, 82
Jordan Clark Haggard, pp. 20, 86, 87 (bottom right), 89 (top)
George Harris, p. 109
Dan Hensley, pp. 165, 167 (bottom left), 168 (bottom right)
Eric Hockman, back cover, pp. 188, 191, 192 (left), 194, 195, 196, 197, 232, 249, 261
Ryan Fred Houston, p. 65 (center)
Seth Hughes, pp. 159, 161
ImagineGnat/Jason Boucher, p. 44 (center)
iStock, pp. 160, 162, 163, 177, 179 (bottom left)
Lisa Janssen, p. 69
JPaks/Joe Tonsager, pp. 192 (right), 193
Wally Kilburg/www.wallykilburg.com, pp. 41, 42, 43, 44 (left, right), 45
Kitsbow Cycling Apparel, p. 27 (left)
Lauf Forks, p. 238 (left)
Kristen Legan, p. 287
Craig Lindner, pp. iv, 4, 47, 48, 49 (top, bottom left), 50 (left, center)
Erin Malone, p. 57 (center, right)
Paolo Martelli, pp. 107, 108 (top left, bottom left, bottom right), 110